THROUGH THE DARK

More Inspiring Stories of Victims, Becoming Survivors
of Domestic Violence

Amberlee Hoagland

For the people who never wished me harm and always saw the good in me, even if I didn't see it myself. I hold you dear.

"One's dignity may be assaulted, vandalized and cruelly mocked, but it can never be taken away unless it is surrendered."

— Michael J. Fox

ACKNOWLEDGMENTS

Many thanks to all the survivors who were brave enough to share their own story in the hopes that it would help another silent victim find her voice, courage, and worth.
You are enough.

* * *

I was 20 years old when I fell in love with him. He was not the usual conservative man I had dated in the past. He had tattoos, was outspoken, and was the first to say an inappropriate joke. In hindsight, we were polar opposites, and it was doomed for failure. The emotional abuse started instantly, through subtle jokes, which I thought was simple playfulness. I was naïve to the fact that degradation comes in many forms, including humor.

Before I can tell my story, some background of my abuser's life needs to be known. He was a victim of child abuse and sexual abuse during his childhood. Shortly before we had met, he had split with his wife and discovered within the first month of our relationship that his son was not biologically his. This man had lots of baggage, to say the least. His bags were full of anger, pain, unrequited love, and low self-esteem.

Ten months into our relationship, we had gone to a Halloween party an hour away from our hometown. We got into an argument, and he left me at the party. I had been drinking, and made the poor choice of kissing an old fling. The next day, I told my ex- boyfriend what had happened after he left me at the party, and to my surprise, he was understanding and apologized for leaving me there.

Two days later, we were having sex. I was kissing him when he suddenly slapped me across my cheek, looked me in the eye, and said to me, "Don't you ever disrespect me like that again!" I had never been more shocked and terrified in my life nor had I ever became teary eyed out of pure fear. At that moment, he gained immense power over me.

From that point on, our sexual life was rattled with abuse. I remember the glare of resentment and anger in his eyes when he hit me the second time, exclaiming, "That is so hot!". I remember my feelings of confusion, fear, violation, along with emotional pain and a deep longing to be loved by him, and to please him. I said nothing. I just succumbed...

His abuse remained in the bedroom, and haunted our sex life for our entire 2 year relationship. I received concussions, my pleas for him to stop hitting me fell on deaf ears or led him to manipulate my emotions with statements like, "Fine! I won't try and make an interesting sex life for us!". It never stopped. My tears got worse, I developed severe anxiety that left me vomiting the moment I woke up every morning, and I spent regular nights locked away in the bathroom sobbing.

I cannot count the number of times I sat at the end of the street with my belongings packed, begging God to give me the strength to drive away and never return.

I continued to sleep with him, longing the intimacy and love that should have reigned over our sex life. I was stuck in a cycle. Sex to receive love only to receive sexual abuse, then clinging evermore, in a desperate attempt to receive the love I was lacking, followed by despair when I was left feeling unloved, and resorting back to sex, in a hope to receive the love through that, just to begin the cycle all over again.

Had he not eventually broken up

with me, there is a great chance I would still be with him. Thankfully, he ended it.

I had no choice but to heal. I slowly began to realize how wrong he was. The curtain was lifted, as I realized I was his emotional and physical punching bag. He poured all of his anger onto me, and I suffered because of it. But, that is over now!

Today I am a mother. I am no longer hit. I mean it when I smile, and I am more discerning of the men I allow in my life.

Please, know your worth. Know that if you choose to give your body to a man, his job is to love it and treat it with care. I learned from that terrible circumstance in my life, and I now have this opportunity to tell a story that may give a woman the strength she needs to drive away and never return, as I should have long ago.

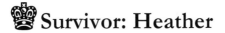 **Survivor: Heather**

EVEN THE DARKEST HOUR HAS ONLY 60 MINUTES
-Morris Mandel

*   *   *

Our abuser, My son Andrew and I,
was a stepfather to Andrew; his bio
father had another family and was
seldom involved. I knew little about
the man, except for the lies he told, but
he seemed so kind and patient with
Andrew, who was a gifted child with an
unusual insight into things and an
insatiable hunger for learning. One of

the nurses at the hospital when he was born, looked at him as he was being weighed and measured and said to me, "This little man's been here before".

It took less than six months before Robert (the stepfather) started to show his true colors, and it was all downhill from then. He started with the isolation from friends, then family; changing the phone number every time a call came for me; criticizing my parenting decisions, even going as far as quoting the Bible to let me know what an evil person I was. How I was going to ruin my son because I was attentive to his love of learning and life; e.g., I wasn't allowed to read to him; he was not allowed to use the computer; his teacher was sent a note saying he was not allowed to go to the library with the class because he couldn't read and his mother had other things to do.

It always escalated ... I have narcolepsy and he used that as an excuse to take my disability money from me. Then he learned that his adoptive father had had a stroke and was put in a nursing home by the father's sister. He insisted that we make twice weekly trips from Pittsburgh, PA to Detroit MI by car (mine), leaving at 2 or 3 a.m. and driving almost eight hours. Once we got there, my son and I would have to sit in the lobby while he visited his non-responsive father for 4 or 5 hours.

On one visit, he came out to the lobby and didn't find us there. He went on a rampage and when he found us in the snack bar, he took the drinks and sandwiches we had on the table and threw them away. "He needs to learn this is not a picnic. He will eat when I

say he can." Andrew was only 5.
These trips also meant that he missed more kindergarten than he attended, which upset Andrew. Finally after four months of these trips, Robert decided to bring his 'father' to our house -- with ulterior motives -- and it was MY job to provide round-the-clock care for this man who was a complete invalid. He would force Andrew to "help" 'grandpa' use his urinal, and other things a child shouldn't. My objections met his fist more than not; and if he chose to, he'd take his anger out on Andrew.

But the day that changed everything ... he told me to go to the store -- you have 30 mins. When I came in the front door afterwards, I noticed that his father was making strange movements with his head and eyes, motioning towards the kitchen/dining room. I could hear muffled sounds and then I heard a WHACK. I was afraid to think the worst because Robert knew that I had never used physical or emotional punishment on Andrew. We'd discuss it ... he understood the concept of actions & consequences. The first 'offense' he'd be told what he did wrong, why it was wrong, what could have happened, etc., and it was a "freebie". And the discussion ended with a consequence if he did the same thing again; no bicycle for a day, cancel an outing we'd planned, etc.

As I turned into the dining room from the kitchen, the first thing I saw was Robert sitting in a chair with a piece of furring strip in his hand, beating it against his palm; and standing in the laundry room doorway a few steps away was my son dressed in just undershorts with his hair dripping wet/

He had the saddest look on his face as he stood with his hands behind his back.

Robert shouts to him, 'Why didn't you do what you were told?' And a timid reply, 'I don't know". "Well, maybe this will help you remember." And he drew back the board and I lunged at him, 'Don't you dare hit him with that.' well, you're too late Momma, I already did, but it didn't seem to help him remember. And he swung it towards my face, grabbing my shirt with the other hand and throwing me to the floor. As I was trying to get my bearings, I heard him order Andrew to turn around and grab your ankles. I couldn't get up in time and I heard him strike Andrew again. Poor little child, he never made a sound, not a whimper. He just stood up, turned around and stood there. Once I got up, I ran over to him and pushed him into the laundry room and sent him to take a cool bath to stop the sting and keep the bruises down.

Robert threw the stick towards me and went out to the garage -- where he'd end up getting drunk, high or both. Once he was out there, I waited because I knew it wouldn't take him long to pass out. Andrew had gotten out of the tub and was drying off when I told him to go to his room, push the dresser in front of his door and keep very quiet, read a book, take a nap. If he tries to get in here, you know how to get out the window and go straight to the neighbors. I had purposely put the picnic table directly beneath his window so he could open it and step right out.

Since Robert didn't allow me to drive (my) car, he always kept the keys hidden and I didn't have time to look for them so I ran about six or seven blocks to the police station. It was CLOSED! sign said call 911 if it's an emergency. I did and went across the street to a restaurant parking lot to wait for an officer. I had to keep out of sight just in case Robert came to and started looking for me ... it had happened before. Finally a cop arrives, I tell my story, which he barely listened to but I finally convinced him my son was in danger and he had to come. He called for backup and we went to the house. The first got Andrew out to the cruiser, then they got Robert in handcuffs to the other car. He went to the local lock-up and we went upstairs to make our report. Photos were taken and the officer escorted us home to get a few things and my car. He told me to go to a friend's house in case he made bail but I said I was going to the hospital first to have Andrew's injuries (bruising) checked out.

He had a series of tests done (which he walked to -- not in a wheelchair), he ate two helpings of spaghetti while we waited between tests; and the doctor said everything checks out fine. Then as he's getting dressed to leave, a child protective caseworker shows up with 2 sheriff deputies. They grabbed me and hauled me to the emergency entrance and she yanks Andrew from the exam room and starts down the hall. I'm kicking, screaming, trying to get away from them and yelled to her, you better have a warrant, b*$%$! She told me she could do what she wanted and didn't need a warrant. In fact, she said, I can give orders to God if I want.

I was bewildered. I had no idea, why this was happening; where they were taking him; and what, if anything, she told him.

Robert was sent to the county jail pending his hearing; he was charged with six felonies, a couple of misdemeanors and I was ASSURED that he was going to go away for a long time. He bailed out after less than a week in jail, by threatening his father to get the money out of his (father's) credit union account. $25K cash. One condition of the bail was he was not to have any contact with me nor come within 100 or so feet of the house or any place I was known to be. The same day he made bail, he calls the house (we didn't have caller ID then) and tells me he's coming to get my Jeep to take his father to the hospital because he was sure I wouldn't take proper care of him.

I told him not to come to the house or I'd call the cops & violate him.

What I didn't know was he'd already gotten the jeep and was sitting in the alley behind the house when he called. Next thing I know he's coming through the back door, which was closed and locked, breaking the exterior door off the hinges and smashing most of the jalousie window. He picks up one of his boots still by the door and throws it right at my face. I saw stars -- literally! He comes over and rips a hank of hair out of the back of my head, scalp attached and starts throwing me from wall to wall to floor. He was 6' and almost 280 lbs.; I was 5'8" and 110 lbs soaking wet with a brick in my pocket. NOT a fair fight! As I laid on the floor, sore and bleeding, he says, 'there's more where that came from if you take your stinking a$# up there and

testify. You'd better just disappear."
And he left.

I called the police but they said they couldn't get out there for a day or so. I was in really bad shape, didn't have a vehicle, so I started walking ... and walking .... from Latrobe, PA to Greensburg; a pretty good hike. I thought I was going in the hospital, but actually it was the mental health unit. Told them what happened, they took me to the ER, diagnosed with a concussion, had stitches in my lip, a broken nose and a black and blue face. Then somehow they managed to get me back to mental health where they admitted me.

Meanwhile, he comes back to the house, finds out from his father that I'd left, and he moved himself back in. He tried to fix the damages he'd done. i was discharged two days later from MH and a police officer took me home, only to find him there. He was told to leave and the officer decided he'd investigate my complaint from the other day. He took photos, talked to his father, saw my injuries and made a report.

But they didn't violate him for almost two weeks. His hearing was in three days. I went to the courthouse ready to testify -- scared as a rabbit -- when someone comes out and tells me I can go home; he'd taken a plea and the matter was settled.

I think he's going to jail, my son can come home and all will be well.

WRONG! He got 11 1/2 - 24 mos. in County. And the best part is, he was granted immediate work release at MY BUSINESS, had my Jeep parked in the jail lot and could leave the prison from

6 am to 6pm, seven days a week to
WORK!!! He was even allowed to keep
a cell phone and was unsupervised
while away from the jail. The store
wasn't open on Sundays, so he'd use
the time to go back to the house and
rest, watch TV or whatever.

I get a call from my attorney who
informs me not to leave the house and
be ready they're coming to arrest you!
For what? For the all the charges
Robert had been charged with. Why?
the judge dropped all the felonies and
only one misdemeanor was charged

I tried to press intimidation of a
witness, breaking & entering,
aggravated and simple assault, violating
a PFA for the incident when he was on
bail, but they laughed and said, you
invited him there, so you must have
knew what was going to happen. Even

the State Attorney General brushed it off as retaliation.

I was released ROR and my attorney. told me they had nothing on me that would stick. This all came about, he said, because the caseworker was pushing the DA to press charges, because she KNEW that I encouraged Robert to "straighten the kid out whatever way he could".

I was told by the PD assigned to me that it's obvious you're guilty here but we're willing to make a deal. Sign the guilty plea and you'll get 6 months probation and then it's over. Oh, and by the way, sign this too. It was a Voluntary Termination of Parental Rights.!!! No way! Well, even though they claimed I was guilty until proven innocent, I knew I had done no harm to my child and I would sign anything that said I did. Well, if you're going to be hard-nosed about it and "make us to go to trial, you're guaranteed to get a nice long State sentence."

I asked, isn't it my RIGHT to have a jury trial; and the reply was, it's much easier this way and if you take up court time, you'll wish you hadn't. I told my attorney that if my son could testify on my behalf, it wouldn't take more than an hour for them to know the truth. A day later, he calls and says, you can't have your son testify. Think of what it would do to him to have to relive all that. The DA says they'll object. And I agreed that he shouldn't have to go thru it all again. But lo and behold on the first day of the trial, who is the first witness? My 7 yr. old son, who was put on the stand for most of the day.

After the morning break, a male juror came back to the judge and says there were two women talking about the case in the break room. And the one woman stood right up and yes, your honor, we were and we have a question. For almost two hours this poor child has been asked question after question and all of his answers refer to a man, a daddy doing all these horrid things to him. If that is the case, why is there a woman sitting at the Defense's table? The judge said, that's irrelevant. You're both dismissed! And the case carried on.

Just six weeks prior to my trial, which was almost a year after the original incident, the Judge had recused herself because she felt that she was still influenced by the media coverage and press to be fair at Robert's trial. Yet, the SAME judge denied my

attorney's motion to recuse claiming
that she hadn't been influenced by
outside sources and could fairly act as
Judge.

Five days of outrageous witness
testimony and the jury goes out.
 verdict comes back, guilty on all
charges. I was handcuffed and
shackled (in high heels and skirt) and
hauled thru the courthouse to be
transported directly to the County Jail
until sentencing, almost two months
later. Bond was immediately revoked,
my car parked on the street, my home
was left with the expectation I would at
least be allowed to go back and get my
'affairs' in order; my father-in-law
sitting in his chair waiting for a meal
and a urinal and two black Labs loose
in the house. It took Dept of Aging

two days to get to the house to "rescue" my father-in-law.

While researching to help Andrew with his Civil Rights case and civil lawsuit, I obtained Robert's court docket. There are four (I think) instances where he went back before this Judge (who recused herself in his case, but heard mine) while still "incarcerated". Four of them were to request "rest time" and she granted him 3 and 4-day furloughs so he could "return to his residence and rest his back". WHAT? You're supposed to be doing time, not going to the spa! He also had his attorney request that she order MY mental health and hospital records from the day I walked there. For what? His trial was over! But she granted the request and ordered them released!.

All in all, I ended up having my sentences made to run concurrent and I ended up having a 5 to 10 yr.. State sentence. I was paroled after 5 yrs., and completed my 5 yrs. of probation without incident. And the really puzzling part, at least to me is, the Judge sentenced me as "an accomplice" on all charges, except one, 'failing to protect'. But when I read the definition of an "accomplice", it says, 'one who aids, abets or assists a perpetrator in the commission of a crime". So, if he (Robert) wasn't charged with any of the crimes, then we do not have a perpetrator; therefore, I was sentenced as an accomplice to a crime that was NOT committed.

If your children are at risk of abuse in any way, GET THEM OUT, even if you don't leave yourself. Send them to grandmas, a friend's, anywhere!

Because once they are abused, you are guilty of "failing to protect".

👑 Survivor: Karen

And one last item: While I was going thru my papers, I found this poem that Andrew wrote and sent to me when I first went to the county jail. We always hear about abuse, DV etc., from the adult victim's perspective. Here's the story as seen through a child's eyes.

He was 7 when he wrote it:

When I was born, my real daddy ran away.
But mom promised she'd always stay.
When I was small, Momma would tell me
My hugs and kisses for you are all free.
She taught me about Jesus and His Love,
Telling me stories about God above.
My mom was with me every day
And guardian angels at night came to stay.
She showed me stuff kids need to know
To be a good person as I grow.
Like always be kind, remember to share;
Brush your teeth. Comb your hair.
Mom worked hard day and night
She always made sure I ate right.
She'd read me books and sing me songs,
Anywhere she went, I went along.
Mostly I had clothes kids wore before,
We got lots of books at the second-hand store.
We didn't have lots, but we weren't poor;

But I always prayed for one thing more.
There was one more thing I wished I had.
I really wanted someone to be my dad.
Finally one day my dreams came true.
Mommy had met somebody new.
We went out to eat and played in the park.
Stop to get ice cream when it got dark.
He said he loved me like I was his son.
I wished for a daddy; now I had one!
I was happy for almost a year,
But things got different when summer got near.
I would see my mom feeling so sad,
The dumbest things got dad real mad.
He started to hit her and Mommy would cry.
I got really scared when I saw her black eye.
She held me real close and hugged me tight,
"Love's not like this. This isn't right."
After we moved to our new house,
I hide in my room, like a little mouse.
I no longer like this guy I called Dad.

He yells and screams and tells me I'm bad.
Me and my mom would try to run away,
But he'd always find us in less than a day.
He puts me in a corner, sends me to bed;
"It will soon be over," one night mom said.
Once dad got mad and broke mom's rules
With a stick he had in his bucket of tools.
Mom tried to stop him before I got hit;
He hit her first and then threw a fit.
I close my eyes, and my bottom hurt.
Mom said, quit it; but he ripped her shirt.
All through the day they continue to fight,
Mom whispers to me, "We'll be safe tonight."
Next thing I see is a big policeman.
I put on my shoes and got in his van.
He put dad in handcuffs and he went too.
All he kept saying, 'is what did I do?'
We told them the story of what he had done;
How I was always in trouble; couldn't have
fun.

The police told us, "Find some place to stay"
He promised to call us sometime today.
Mom hugged and kissed me, said, we're okay
And went to the hospital for an x-ray.
But here comes a lady, this doesn't feel right.
She took me from mommy that awful night.
"I'll always love you", I could hear Mommy say,
I couldn't hug her, they just took me away.
I rode in a car to a dark, strange place.
Mom's kisses and lots of tears on my face.
Where is my mom? Is she all right?
I cried in that bed every night.
Your mommy hurt you;
I said, it's a lie.
I just want to see her; feel like I will die.

. . . .

THROUGH MY CHILD'S EYES

I talked to Jesus with tears in my eyes,
God, can you hear little boys in my size?
Mommy's gone; they say daddy's in jail.
I want to call her or send her some mail.
'Your mom doesn't want you back',
They lie as they hand me clothes in a sack.
Finally one day I get to see her again.
I hug her and cry, 'where have you been?'
She promised she loves me forever and ever
She'll fight to get me; she'd not quit — never!
Two times a month my mom would come,
Every time I hoped she could take me home.
I got the bad news in the first grade,
The Judge's decision had finally been made.

Mom's going to prison for lots of years.
She tells me to pray, but I don't think He
hears.
I have to move again and again;
Another new house, new school, no friends.
I don't think it's fair what they say,
My mom never hurt me in any way.
She calls me to say stay healthy, be brave,
Do your homework, and always behave.
I'm trying real hard to do the best I can
So when I'm grown I will be a nice man.
Now, there is one person I hope I don't see:
It's that monster that hurt mommy and me.
I love you, Mommy, I want to shout out loud
And I promise when I'm grown you will be
proud.

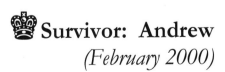 **Survivor: Andrew**
(February 2000)

AMBERLEE HOAGLAND

*   *   *

I met my abuser in the early part of the year 2001. We were just dating off and on for a while. In March of 2003, we decided to get married at the Magistrate's Office. The first year was okay. We were adjusting to each other and also raising my two daughters from previous relationship.

I noticed that he was drinking more and more and also started doing drugs. I sat him down and had a talk with him and told him nothing good comes out of doing drugs and alcohol. Then he purchased a gun claiming to protect our family. He kept the gun hidden so no one could find it. I work at a hospital at that time and I met a lot of people and became close with my co-workers. At the end of the day, he would be parked in the hospital parking lot watching me as I get off from work and go to my car. As soon as I got home, he would questioning me who was the man you were talking too. He told me right then and there that he doesn't want his wife talking to another man.

There were many things that I have been through with this man and it changed my life completely. He put the gun beside my head and dared me to pull it. Then he told me he was just playing. There were plenty of times when we would wake up, he would arguing with me. He would hit me, slap me, bite me and when it come to having sex, saying no was not an option. I would just have to take it. He would 'check me to see if I had been with anyone else.. He accused me of being with my father, my brothers, cousins, coworkers and anyone else he could think of.

I would go to work with bruises on me. One day I was in the hospital chapel and he came in and locked the door and started attacking me because I would not buy him breakfast. He was choking me, pulling my hair and slapping me. The security unlocked the door and pulled him off of me and told him never to come back. The damage was done because everyone knew what happened and what type of man he was.

Two weeks later I was coming home from work with my two daughters and my best friend was in front of me and I honked the horn and we pulled over and we talked in front of a recycle building. Someone went back and told my husband that I was standing in outside talking to a man. Before I could even get home, he had gotten off work rushed home and accused me of sleeping with my friend. Next he slapped me, choked me and pushed my head into a picture frame. Glass broke everywhere. I took a piece of glass and I stabbed him in the arm to protect myself.

The police got involved, Child Protective Service ordered him to stay away from the house but that didn't work. A month later, I came home and he was in the house. He had cut my clothes, broke my things Threw my daughters toys away. Right then and there we were fighting like cats and dogs. I got in the car and he took a cylinder block and threw it in the car windshield and said when my daughter turns eighteen he was going to rape her. Right then I had get out. In the year of 2007, I went to the local Coastal Women's Shelter and they helped me get a restraining order. My brother and father invited me to move back home. He had me so isolated from my family that I wouldn't go visit them or anything. I would come home straight from, work and stay in the house.

I packed our things and put the rest in storage. We were back home with my father and my girls were out of danger. There were many nights I cried myself to sleep because of what I allowed to happen to me. to my daughters.. I sought counseling for us. It was a process. It was a lot of tears but those moments meant we were getting on with our lives.

In July of 2010, my husband came in my father's house to talk to me. He got mad and threw weights through my truck window and car windows. I called the police and I pressed charges. The day we went to court, the judge told him to stay away from the house. After I left court I went to the courthouse to file for my divorce and came out to find my truck keyed up.. I went to the magistrate and they told me that if I didn't see him doing it, it was nothing that they can do.

In September of 2010, I was granted my divorce. The happiest day of my life. He had no reason to bother me because I was no longer his wife. I was still going to counseling but he seems like it was at a standstill.

Everywhere I would go it seemed like I would see him. When I go the park she shows up. I go to the grocery store, he shows up, and it was very depressing. I would literally get upset and be in a bad mood. One night I was looking at a show and this woman was talking about a man having control over a woman. She was saying every time you would see this man and you get upset that means he still has control of him. Let it go and let God.

Right then I had to forgive myself and forgive him too. When I did that my life changed amazingly. When I see him it doesn't bother me anymore. Through family support and counseling and trusting in God I am now a survivor.

Through years of counseling, sharing my story, and being a mother, it has gotten easier for me. I let every day be better than the next day. I changed my lifestyle to a point where I am comfortable. I spend more time with my daughters and teaching them the signs of abuse. I am a survivor and I pray for those you are going to this would get out immediately. That is the first step and the rest will come easier just day by day. It is hard work but it is worth getting your life back and being happy.

Do it for yourself and if you have kids do it for them. Break that pattern.

👑 **Survivor: Tracy**

There weren't very many people that were kind to me when I was in high school. However, there was this one boy that was super sweet to me. He would carry my books to the bus for me. I ended up marrying a different guy

when I was seventeen and still in high
school. Several years went by after
graduation, and we had two daughters
together.

I was on the Internet in 2004, and
this ad popped up for a Classmates
website. The internet was new to me at
this time. I thought about if there were
anyone that I hadn't seen since my high
school days, and this boy had come to
mind. I wondered where he ended up
and if he was happy in his life. I typed
his name in on this website, and he was
on there. I decided to join so I could
talk to him. We e-mailed each other for
a while. Then, we later talked on the
phone and decided we wanted to
reunite.

In June of 2006, I left my husband of fifteen years. We had grown apart over the years, and I was very unhappy for the last ten years of our marriage. In October of 2006, our divorce became final. I had been living with my boyfriend since June.

As I try to recall things, I have a difficult time remembering details. I believe it was my natural response to the extreme amount of fear that I felt deep within my mind and heart.

The abuse started at the end of 2006. He became angry with my friend that was over, and he started to physically hurt her. I ran out of the back door of my house. I opened up my truck door with plans to honk the horn in order to get the attention of the rescue squad across the road. He caught up with me, grabbed me by the shoulder, and pushed me down to the ground. I was in shock at what just happened. That was only the beginning of his control over me.

There were several more incidents that occurred after this one for the next year. He would get angry with me over things that weren't my fault and slap me. He yelled at me over the littlest things. I got to the point where I didn't want to talk to him in fear I would say something to set him off. He struggled with his own inner demons. At one point of our relationship, he believed and acted like he had multiple personalities. He attempted to self-medicate with alcohol in order to escape his thoughts. He chose to consume rum or vodka in large quantities. He would have fits of rage and break whatever was in his path. There was one incident that he held a knife up to my throat while saying, "I will end you" in front of my daughters.

On October 30, 2007, the house we were renting burned to the ground. I refer to this time in our lives as a blessing in disguise. It allowed us to move into a new neighborhood where I was surrounded by distant relatives and supportive people. I gained the courage to kick him out of our lives by the end of 2008. I began to regain control of my life.

Then, in March of 2009, my world was turned upside down. My older daughter's boyfriend called me and told me about a secret he kept for her that he struggled with for a while. Jacob had repeatedly raped my daughter, Erika, over the course of six months. He stole her virginity! I immediately contacted the Kentucky State Police and reported this crime. The following year was filled with meetings with the county's prosecuting attorney and court dates. Finally, in April of 2010, Jacob was sentenced to twelve and a half years in

prison for sexually abusing my
daughter.

I discovered through therapy at a
local rape crisis center that he didn't
rape only Erika; he also repeatedly
raped me. It's referred to as Intimate
Partner Rape. Domestic Violence and
Sexual Abuse are often connected.

All of these events in my life were
very traumatic! I have had so many
dark days! But, in the end, I have found
strength within me that I never knew
existed. I would not be the person I am
today if I hadn't lived through those
experiences.

I wouldn't have the passion within

me to help others who have gone through similar situations. I am living proof that domestic violence doesn't define you, and there is always a way out!

God Bless Y'all!

A Victim No More

Survivor: Laura Lynn

*   *   *

When I was 21 years old I met a
man who became my boyfriend. I was
in love not knowing he would soon
become my worst nightmare. I was
young and blind to the emotional abuse
until it became physical. I lived out of
state, on the other side of the country.
All my family and friends were 3000

miles away. I felt helpless. I had no one
and nowhere to go.

I remember one day we were
walking down the boardwalk and he
got upset and began to throw me
around, someone noticed and called the
cops. I was naive didn't want him to go
to jail. I did everything I could to cover
his actions. I even went as far as to tell
the police that the marks on my neck
(from being choked) were hickies, that
my guy would never hurt me
intentionally. He loved me.

I bailed him out and we made up
and we moved to get a fresh start. We
were happy, we were in love, we got
pregnant, I was overjoyed. I was always
told I'd never have kids, This was my
miracle, my reason for living. We were
getting ready to move into our own
home, closer to my family, things were

changing, like he always said they would. We'd argue, he'd erupt, I began to think this was normal, I silently took what I had coming. I never told my friends or family because I was this brash girl who didn't need any help, instead I kept quiet about the years of abuse I had endured at his hands.

I remember one night he came home from being out drinking, I had been working a 16 hour shift and got home right after him, I asked him to make me a peanut butter and jelly sandwich because I was tired and pregnant been working all day and going to do it the next day as well, he kicked the bathroom door down, threw the sandwich at me and started hitting my face, I was covered in soap in the shower in the fetal position trying to protect the child I had growing inside me, the most precious gift I could ever

receive. He pulled me from the shower
and started kicking me, with everything
I had I tried to protect my stomach and
the life inside.

At my next doctor's appointment I
would find out my attempts to protect
my child were fruitless, they told me
they could not find the heartbeat, and
perhaps we had miscalculated the date,
they said I couldn't be 4 months
pregnant. Being that we'd moved 3
times since finding out I was pregnant I
had paper work from several doctors
confirming how far along I was. They
told me to come back in a week, I
couldn't wait. I knew something wasn't
right. I went to the ER where they told
me I had lost my baby.

My world crumbled. I got home,
and I made him leave, I had not told
anyone in my family the horror I was

living with, so instead I got a payday advance bought him a bus ticket and told him to leave. It infuriated him, I told him to leave. He made sure he got to beat me up one more time, breaking my nose and 3 fingers, but He did leave fairly easily considering the hell I had put up with for the last two years.

This monster that I allowed into my life, and into my heart had manipulated me and beaten me to the point I was a shell of my former self. Had I not stayed with him, had I not kept allowing him back in my life, had I not been so concerned about staying together for my child perhaps my child would still be here today. There is not a day that doesn't pass that I don't think about my little girl. Instead of remembering birthdays I now have the torture of remembering the day I put

my child, my little miracle, my Reia
Sunshine Murphy into the cold ground.

I live with the guilt that I could have
prevented this life changing event, that
had a been a stronger person I would
be celebrating my 3 year olds birthday
next month. If I could talk to the girl I
was then I would try to tell her how
precious life is, and not just the child
inside, but hers as well. That she
deserved something more, something
better that no one deserves to be
treated with such violence and no one
deserves to live in fear. I would tell
myself there is a such thing as true love
that it hasn't been found yet by you.
But she wouldn't have listened.

Sometimes it takes living through a
tragic event to make you a stronger. I
have sisters, cousins, nieces I hope that
would feel safe enough to talk to me or

someone if they're ever in a position I was. I wish I'd have been strong enough to talk to someone while I was going through this, maybe the outcome would have been different. But since you can't change the past, you grow from it. I'm stronger than I've ever been. I know my worth and I will never be in that position again.

I hope anyone who reads this can realize there is help out there, there are people who can help. Tell someone, talk to someone, don't suffer in silence. You deserve the world don't settle for less.

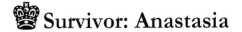 **Survivor: Anastasia**

*   *   *

Sometimes when I close my eyes I still feel like I am caught up in the whirlwind of being the wife of someone who was and is physically violent. I met my husband about seven or eight years ago when I returned to Trinidad to pursue my degree. I saw him at church and thought he was a fine specimen. We'd exchange pleasantries but we didn't actually have a conversation until I asked someone for his number.

We spent an entire night exchanging messages. The next night he messaged me and asked what I was doing. As I was not at home at the time I figured it would have been out of his way, but he still visited anyway. Two days later he invited me on a drive down South with him as he had to head that way for work and I accepted. We went to church that Sunday together and we made plans to meet up the following week.

Needless to say we began spending more time together. We were almost inseparable. The only times we didn't spend together was when he was out of the island for work, otherwise you saw us everywhere. He introduced me to his family and some of his friends. We had a pretty good relationship. However, if anyone asked him if we were together he'd always say no.

In May of 2009 he told me it was best if we called it quits, that he could not give me what I was looking for and I'd be better off with another man. I didn't question it nor did I fight him on it. I had enough to keep me busy between work, school and my duties as a Warrant Officer (WOII) in the Trinidad & Tobago Cadet Force (TTCF).

The following month I found out I was pregnant. I told him and his response to me was that he was going to deny it until the child was born as it would put his job in jeopardy. He worked for the church, and sexual relations outside of marriage was a breach of his contract. I told him I wasn't ready to have a baby yet. I was 23 at the time and really more concerned with finishing my degree. I also could not agree with him staying quiet in his corner while I was left to endure the hot water alone. He told me if I had an abortion he would never speak to me again. I told him okay and as far as I was concerned that was the end of the conversation.

I did have an abortion. One which went horribly wrong. During my bouts of morning sickness at work and feeling sick, the doctor in charge of A&E was who looked out for me. I told no one I had the abortion. One day while I was at my husband's (then boyfriend's) home I began to bleed profusely. It seemed like a miscarriage and I left it at that. In the days that followed I bled and bled with no end in sight. I eventually spoke with my friend the doctor who advised me on what to do. As I had to have an ultrasound done to determine what was going on, a rumor started spreading around the hospital that I was pregnant for him and had had an abortion.

Eventually that issue was rectified and the connection between my husband and I intensified. Eventually he started to talk about marriage. I didn't take him seriously until I saw the ring. So in essence I can say he proposed on a Friday evening and we were married the following Monday morning (November 2009), although the dates and everything were decided upon before he officially proposed.

It was to be a simple wedding between him and I. However, the day

before the wedding he invited his
family and friends and so it was really
all about him at the wedding. I didn't
think much of it then, but now I often
wonder…

We moved in together and I
continued between work, school and
my duties in the TTCF. Later that year,
my sister visited and he refused to allow
her to stay at our apartment citing how
it would look if she stayed there with
her boyfriend who she wasn't married
to knowing the role he held in the
church. I said okay and asked a friend if
she could stay at his house to which he
agreed. That turned into a big issue as I
was back and forth between his house
and home with my sister and her
boyfriend.

In January 2010 I found pictures
of him kissing another woman on his

phone. I actually went into a very quiet state and refused to get out of bed for a couple of days. One morning I woke up and found him with my journal in his hand reading the reason why I stopped speaking to him. He told me we would talk about it when I was ready. I told him that he created that monster so deal with it. Later that day I took off my rings and left them on the bed. When I came home, renewed after having a chat with my Branch President (Pastor) willing to try it again, my rings were gone. When I asked him for them he said that if I could rally as a married woman without my rings then do so. I stopped going anywhere with him and when people asked for me he would tell them I was sick. His sisters eventually visited the house unbeknownst to him and told me in no uncertain terms that he was in fact a womanizer, and that the reason why they came was to find out if I was pregnant since he kept saying I was sick.

A few days later he went into my bag while I was asleep and stole my journals. His brother was staying in the house with us and while we were scuffling over the journals, he gave his brother his computer bag which had in the journals and he left the house with them. That was the last time I ever saw those journals.

In that altercation he squeezed my arm which had a nasty black and blue welt on it. For that entire week I wore long sleeved shirts to work in an effort to cover it up. One co-worker even remarked that she hoped my husband wasn't hitting me and that was the reason why I was in long sleeves all week. The Friday of that week, my friend the doctor passed by the hospital to drop off a package for me. He touched my arm and I flinched. He asked me what was wrong. I played it off as best I could, but when he saw the mark, he suggested I have one of the doctors in the clinic see to it, which I did. I also made a police report at the station.

After my husband found out I had made a police report against him, he became enraged and one Sunday after church he sent a message to me via the Branch President informing me that all my stuff was outside so come and get them. I simply turned up at the apartment with a police escort and left. His family were also infuriated that I would have the nerve to take him to court. He started telling people that I had someone hit me and then make a report against him of domestic violence. Needless to say, my husband was summoned to court. The magistrate sent us for counseling. We had a one on one session with a probation officer who sent a report back to the magistrate. The magistrate was shocked that we were this way after a mere three months of marriage. She told us to work it out and that she did not want to see us back in front of her.

I was staying at a friend's apartment. His house was three streets over from where I was staying. My husband picked me up one evening and because I would not let him see the inside of the apartment he refused to take me where we were going. I eventually let him see the inside of the apartment.   During that time apart, we started dating again and one day I came home from work and the woman who I saw my husband kissing in the pics on his phone was there. I told her she needed to leave.

He told me I was home at him and could not ask anyone to leave. He blocked my path, walked her down the stairs and locked her in his truck. I was flattened to say the least and snapped. I went downstairs and was going to open the door and pull her out the truck. I was on the verge of shattering the passenger side window.

He dragged me through the street and told me to stop with my Beetham behavior. I called my Branch President who came and saw everything. So it was then clear to him that I was in fact not lying about his behavior as my husband was leading everyone to believe. The next day my husband messaged to ask me how my hand was doing and if I was okay. He even came to the apartment to see how I was doing. I was shocked but took it to mean that he really wanted the relationship, so I gave in to him that time as well.

Fast forward a few months later, we had another blow up. I had moved back in with him by then. I started sleeping in the next room. He was fired from his job at the church for his insubordination, but blamed it on me. He decided he needed a break and had gone to the USA on holiday to spend some time with his sister and her family. I was really missing him and trying my best to keep it together while I still had to manage dealing with work and school. About that time as well I found out I was pregnant again, but I guess with the stress and pressure of the last abortion that went wrong, I had a miscarriage.

I told him about it and he came back. The thing is when he came back,

I didn't want him around me. I went to Barbados to spend two weeks with my mom and upon my return a can of worms opened. I was sick with dengue and needed to leave home to register for school. I asked my husband for my ID card as he had it. He told me he didn't. It turned into a shouting match. Eventually he hog tied me and put a pillow over my face saying it was either I took my tie up quietly or fight and make it worse.

He only calmed down when the Branch President arrived at the house. I needed to get my medication and so the Branch President told me to leave the house and get some fresh air to calm myself and offered to take me for the medication. When I returned, my husband had barred me from entering the house. I spent the night at my Branch President's home in the hope that he would calm down and I would at the very least get my things the next day. I went so far as to let my husband know that my cycle was on me and I needed my stuff. He did not so much as budge. I spent five days in the same clothes until my mom was able to send some money for me to get some toiletries, clothes, etc. I made countless reports at the station. The police went with me to the apartment and each time he would not answer the door. They told me there was nothing they could do if he didn't open the door. I made a report at court and was issued with an order to get my things, but mister literally disappeared and so was not served. It took me about two months to get my stuff.

So here I was out of the marital home again, back and forth between friends. No job, couldn't go to school since he had kept my stuff from me and so I could not start the semester. A few weeks later I found out I was pregnant again. I told him and his question to me was how did he know it was his. That he wanted a paternity test. I remember the night I told him I spent crying on his couch as I had gone to the apartment to have that conversation with him face to face. The next day I made up my mind to borrow the money to have another abortion. Fortunately, I couldn't get the money borrowed.

Our anniversary was coming up and I planned a trip for us to Tobago in the hopes that we could reconcile, put everything behind us and have a family. We went and it was pretty okay. Following our return to Trinidad, I could not get out of bed. Morning sickness hit me for six. I used to

literally spend my days curled up in bed.
I guess when he realized how sick I was
and couldn't do anything for myself, he
came off his high horse and turned into
the husband I always wanted. Come to
think of it, that is the only time during
our marriage he acted like a husband.

Our daughter was born July of the
following year (2011) in Barbados. He
kept singing that he wanted a paternity
test. I eventually told him to go ask his
father for a paternity test to make sure
he was in fact his father. After that he
stopped. I however was in a totally
different frame of mind. I could not
stomach him touching our daughter, as
I somehow used to see in him in my
mind's eye abusing her the same way he
abused me and I always feared that he
would do her something. I returned to
Trinidad in September for her
christening but only for ten days. I told

him I needed to sort things out and see where we went from there. He told people that he left me at home and when he returned home the house was empty and that I had taken his child and left. Mind you, he was the one who took us to the airport.

When I went back to Trinidad to finish study, I went back minus our daughter as I still did not trust him. And as I had no job I had no way of looking after her since he refused to contribute to her in any way whatsoever. We had another argument one Sunday morning. I was again sleeping in the other bedroom and as I did not trust him as far as I could spit, the night before I had locked the door before I went to bed. He kept some of his clothes in that bedroom and as he wanted to go out that night and couldn't get in he was annoyed to say the least. That Sunday morning he began taking the lock off of the door. I asked him if he was losing his marbles and he started advancing toward me with the screwdriver he had in his hand. I was standing with my back against the couch. The only thing in my hand was a cup of tea and so I threw it at him. He tied me up again & almost suffocated me. I packed up my things for good one last time and moved into my dad's home. I stopped talking to him and had nothing to do with him for almost a year. He did not know where I was and was all over Trinidad looking for me like a madman, sending me messages about how sorry he was and he wanted his family.

Again against my better judgment, I called him and we started seeing each other again. I would visit him, but I never allowed him to visit me. We had another blow up again. This time over his lack of contributing to our daughter's well being and his lack of interest in her. He dragged me through the road, cuffed me across my face, literally body slammed me in the garage which resulted in permanent damage to my back. You name it, he did it to me. I eventually cut all ties with him.

He started coming around again, showing an interest in our daughter and moved in with me at the beginning of last year as much as my heart wasn't in it. Last year we made arrangements for our daughter to visit Trinidad for the summer, so we could all spend some time together. Two weeks prior to our daughter's arrival in Trinidad, we went to a football match and I was chatting with a guy whom I know from school. I guess he didn't like it and he started to rant and rave on the way home about my disrespect toward him I ignored him really and so he cuffed me across my mouth. I ended up with three stitches in my mouth.

I remember feeling the blood pooling in my mouth like water. I finally managed to get out of the car and went home. He called my Mom and told her that he didn't know what I was going to do. I left home to seek medical attention. He shadowed me all the way to the clinic and when my name was called to be seen by the doctor, he walked in. When the security guard asked him who he was, he proudly said, 'I am her husband'. When I was asked how the mishap happened, I lied again as I had done so many times in the past and said a fight broke out where we went to watch the football match and I was an unfortunate bystander. After we left the clinic, while walking to get transportation home, he said to me that he didn't mean to hit me but I made him so mad sometimes. I didn't have much to say to him after that, and as my silence usually drive him crazy, he moved out of the house a week later.

About two weeks later our daughter arrived in the island. She was however accustomed to seeing us together and kept asking when her daddy was coming back, so he decided to move back in while she was there. I told him stay in his corner and I'll stay in mine. One night he went through my laptop and saw some messages between a friend and I on Facebook. He then told me it was either him or my friend. I told him to not let the door hit him on his way out. He then began threatening me telling me it was either my friends whom he did not approve of or him, otherwise he was going to apply for a divorce. I told him to please do so, that I was going outside and by the time I came back in he should have packed his things to be on his way.

I picked up his car keys to get our daughter's car seat and some other stuff from in the car. He became enraged and came at me. He cuffed me across my face, backed me in a corner and slit the palm of my hand with a kitchen knife. When I saw my hand in pieces and considering our daughter was in the next room it woke something up in me. Someone called the police (I still don't know who did), they came and took him into custody. He spent the weekend in prison.

I eventually was granted a protection order. He appeared in court and asked for the case to be postponed citing he was seeking legal counsel. We appeared in court again, him with his lawyer, me without as I could not afford one. I was assigned one through legal aid, but she was not interested in my case to say the least. The magistrate eventually withdrew my protection order as his lawyer argued that he had not contacted me in two months. I told the magistrate to please caution him about turning up at my house after that. I knew while the protection order was in effect he would not disobey the order which stated that he was to be 100 feet away from me and the house at all times. As soon as the order was withdrawn he began calling me, sometimes three times for the day. I made reports but because he now lived outside of the jurisdiction there was nothing the police could do about it.

When the protection order was withdrawn I didn't feel safe at home. Every noise I would jump. I started to get anxiety attacks. I started to black out. I couldn't eat or sleep. I felt like I was alone in my corner. I had lost friends because of him and there was literally no one I could call. I spent the week after our court hearing house sitting for a friend so it worked out thankfully that I was not in the house. Our anniversary was on 16th November. I remember going to church that Sunday and thinking I had wasted the last six years of my life. The next morning I hopped on a plane and have not been in Trinidad since. I told no one I was leaving. But I guess there are some who believe they need to keep my husband abreast of all that I do and so he called and messaged asking where I was, wondering if I was okay, that he wanted to see me, he was concerned. I took it all with a pinch of salt. That lasted all of nine days and then he resumed his usual; I am selfish, indifferent, inconsiderate, a baddist, a whore and the list goes on.

At the beginning of this year, he told me I needed to 'woman up', take responsibility for my child and stop letting my mother manipulate me. I asked him while I do that what would he be doing as last I checked I was the parent working her ass off and sacrificing for the child he did not want in the first place.

I told him in no uncertain terms to go screw himself. That was in January. I have not spoken to him since. I have since blocked him on social media. I have since employed a call blocker. I do see if and when he calls but his calls do not come through as in my phone does not ring when he does call, but rather leaves a notification informing me of such. He still continuously calls. He has told everyone who would listen to him that I am the worst human being this side of the western hemisphere, but I am used to it by now.

Our daughter is no worse for wear. It took a while after the incident in August to get her back to where she is now. She kept saying for a long time that her mummy has a cut in her hand that hurts and the police took her daddy.

She acted out for a few months well. She's okay now, enjoying life like the average three and a half year old should. I am not altogether there yet. I still don't like people to touch me. I cringe each time someone attempts to hug me. It's not as bad as it used to be, but it's still there. Before I left Trinidad, I started counseling with both the Coalition Against Domestic Violence and Victim Support. For a long time I blamed myself for my 'failed' marriage. It took me a long time to believe that I in fact was not to blame and that my husband is sick. Two marriages ending the same way, with the same issues on his part says a lot. He is convinced that he is attracted to women who have mental issues. He has told people that I am mad.

Even while we were together, I asked him to attend counseling with me and he refused. He always had the notion that there is nothing wrong with him and since he has already been married, he has more experience than me in that field.

I have lost friends, given up things that were important to me, been kicked out of the TTCF, alienated myself from family and things I enjoy doing, all for a man who couldn't appreciate it, while he gave up nothing for me or our marriage and made certain I knew this. There was NOTHING I would not have done for my husband because I was in love with him. And although I still do love him and hope that one day he can get the help he needs to make himself a better man, I am not in love with him any longer. If I don't ever see him again, it would be too soon.

I feel violated, I feel cheap, I feel discarded, I feel like no one would have any use for me ever again and I would never be able to be in a 'normal' relationship again.

Despite all that however, like an ass I still worry about him, I still think about him occasionally. I have no idea if I am a divorced woman yet or not considering he did say he was going to apply for a divorce. I still don't trust him around my daughter and have taken steps in ensuring he cannot be with her on his own. I know I still have a long way to go in healing. At times I do miss the companionship and having someone to talk with, or even having someone to come home to and do stuff for, but all things considered I trust no one, and in retrospect I guess I have no one to blame for that but myself.

Many times we hear stories of domestic violence in households and ask or think why didn't the woman leave. Sadly, that is easier said than done. There are so many factors which have to be considered when leaving and leaving for good, especially if children are involved. I am a victim of domestic violence. Some days are better than others, but I take comfort in knowing I can make it through this as well; one day at a time.

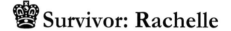 **Survivor: Rachelle**

*   *   *

I never wanted children until I thought I'd found the man of my dreams. My life was going to be set just great, and I was going to be a proud mommy, wife, and daughter.. Little did I know I was in for the most physical, mental, emotional pain I've ever endured, and to this day I don't know how I'm still here. Let's go back to that "man of my dreams". I dated him for over 5 years and was introduced to him through his mother who was a regular at my job and I knew he had a rough past but I believe in change and seeing the best in people. I wish I wasn't so forgiving, and vulnerable.

I believed everything he told me about being changed and he was going to be all I had yearned for as a husband, and father to our daughter. Yes, he was in jail and prison but never for anything violent so I thought nothing of it. We moved in together and got pregnant on a cold January night. We started arguing over nothing. He got defensive when I brought up his drug usage which he thought I was oblivious to. He'd scream in my face; push; slap; spit on me.

During the first couple months of pregnancy he'd stolen around $700 and

disappeared after an argument and
hitting me. He shows up a day or two
later dirty and exhausted because he
had gone on a crack and heroin (and
god knows what else) binge with that
$700 I had saved to put toward
furnishing my baby's room. Gone like
that.

   I was so upset, disgusted, beside
myself. I cannot put it into words. He
cried and apologized begging for
forgiveness. Said it'd never happen
again, he lost control he was wrong and
all that song and dance, and me being
naive, pregnant, fearful of being alone,
stayed positive and thought we can get
through this. I'll forgive him, and I
wanted to for me and the baby. At this
time he was working and I was home
pregnant.

He was a hothead, and drug addict, and he was hitting me regularly, and verbally abusing me to no avail. I had lost myself and hated him and myself for not having courage to leave because it was my house and how dare he, But oddly enough I still believed in him. Praying every minute for things to get better and him to go back to who I fell in love with. He didn't think he was ever wrong. Apologized but just repeatedly hurt me physically and mentally/emotionally. Over and over again. I was only living for the baby I had growing inside me and, I was more in love with her then anything so I put up with everything you could possibly imagine.

Our baby girl was born 8 pounds and healthy via emergency c section. When I became coherent hours later my mommy was only one beside me.

He was nowhere to be found after he
held her and whatnot apparently he
went through my stuff found the bank
card, and went drug hunting. To this
day my mom won't tell me what
happened but says she will never
forgive him for what he did in hospital
while I was in surgery and recovery.
Something went on and he tried to get
my mom kicked out of hospital that's
all I know.

He lost his job the day I had her.
He spent whatever money we did have
and I remember him looking so messed
up and there was nothing I could do. I
was dying emotionally and was just cut
in half for this c section. He didn't care.
He did stay in room with me whole
time I was kept in hospital 5 days.
Taking 3 hour "smoke breaks". I was
left alone with my baby, saying to her
when I looked into her innocent eyes-

mommy loves you baby -I'll never hurt you-I'll try to give you the world you are my heart now-you are me-I live for you-I love you.

We got home eventually and my parents live close so if I needed anything or questions, I'd call. He ended up stealing all my medicine they gave me for pain.

He got into it with me about something and took my car and left. I believe it was about 2 days I reported car stolen but cops never did anything when he did stuff because they said my address is on his license so legally he can just come back. Eventually he did and about 5 days home still having staples holding me together I had taken the beating of a lifetime.

I believe he was drunk I don't recollect exactly but nothing should trigger that type of reaction no matter what.

I remember the baby in her little snug a bunny bouncer over there sound asleep as I looked up before my eyes were punched and swollen shut, seeping, bleeding everywhere. I was screaming-NO PLEASE STOP, I love you, I'm sorry, the baby please stop, don't kill me. Saying anything to get him to stop. I'm the one that was screaming that I was sorry and I loved him, to save my own life as I took kicks to my stapled stomach thinking that was the end. I fell limp curled into the fetal position, my head, back, legs being kicked full force stomped on, spit on punched, smacked, backhanded. All while he was screaming obscenities that

I definitely cannot repeat. I was a bitch with every hit I took.

I was literally black, not blue, bruised and battered I couldn't even call anyone or do anything. He wouldn't let me move in fear of the cops and anyone seeing me because if anyone had you would know something wasn't right. So I had a towel or blanket over my face and head as I talked to the baby or fed her because I didn't want to scare her as I Knew I looked like a monster. I couldn't see it fully myself because my eyes were basically sealed shut from swelling I remember trying to wipe leakage from both eyes and barely being able to walk, sit or lay due to every orifice of my body being swollen, sprained, broken, bruised or whatever I was in agony all over, bedridden, hunched holding my stomach hoping my insides were ok.

The staples still in but not looking
pretty.

Eventually I healed and his
mother was over. Mind you no one had
known what he had just done. They
ended up turning against me ganging
up on me not giving me my baby to
hold and take away from them. I called
my parents and my neighbor and
eventually things were semi settled. Not
long after that his mother shows up to
my neighbor who was watching the
baby for a short time and attempted to
take the baby.

My mom knew something was
wrong and sent over my dad and he
says "she reeked of vodka". That turned
into a whole mess and out of spite she
called child protective services. After
several calls they took my baby because
they thought I was unfit for being with

him and she was present when I
endured the abuse.

He refused whatever treatment
was recommended to get her back. I
never lost the privilege of seeing her
but she resides with my father now and
they are legally adopting her because of
how he has destroyed my home and me
in general. I think that pain is worse
than any physical injury you can endure.
I'm left empty and dead inside by the
loss of my baby. Tears fall from my
eyes as I write this no matter how much
time passes this pain will never go
away. My only remedy is prayer at this
point.

Aside from mental and physical
damage My doors all have holes or are
just ripped from hinges, there is blood
stains on curtains, carpet. He's
shattered my glass doors in the china

cabinet, holes in the floor, my glasses I need to see are broken from being punched in the face. My couches are torn and stained from blood. He managed to get both my vehicles impounded. I cry at the drop of a dime. I'm afraid to be around people, have no friends. Embarrassed of my once beautiful home and self. He just tore me and all I had to nothing. I believe if I had my home fixed up, a vehicle, and intense therapy and help I could thrive and find myself once again I can't catch up on bills since he got me so behind from stealing from me. I take it one step at a time.

My family lost their trust in me because I stayed with him but you only understand how DV is if you've survived it like me. As I am writing this I re-live the terror and cry uncontrollably. I sleep with her baby blankys that I once swaddled her in, and as I can still smell the slightest scent of baby I cry out for her and pray for my life to get better and for some miracle. I have to believe I lived through this for a reason. Even if it's just to tell you, or save some girl out there that can get out before I did. Every day I get stronger. I'm still here and fighting and I know that God has plans for me.

👑 **Survivor: Stephie**

* * *

It was winter of 2009 I had just gotten out of a 5 Year Marriage 9 months previously. I started going on a dating site "Plenty of Fish" And started talking to Tony and Brandon around the same time. I decided to meet with Tony and we dated for a couple of months. During that time it felt like we were just friends with benefits, someone to party with and I felt like a used toilet paper. I got tired of feeling that way and was looking for something more long term. Brandon was always on my case about who I was hanging out with. I reassured him I was hanging out with just a friend. Tony and I were just friends with benefits and I didn't think I needed to explain to Brandon our situation just that I was with a friend.

New Years Day 2010 I broke up things with Tony as I found out he never wanted a relationship with me, only sex. On this day Brandon found out that I had stayed the night with Tony and was furious, we had a big fight on our cell phones/text messaging. So after I broke things off with Tony, I then chose to make things right with Brandon and meet him for the first time as he was getting impatient with me about us hanging out as I always had an excuse or I was at work.

Brandon and I were wrong for each other from the start. At the end of our first date he asked me "So are you going to be my girlfriend or what?! When he asked me in such a condescending and a very rude tone; I felt like I was obligated to tell him yes, so I did.

The second date with Brandon I wanted to introduce him to a girlfriend of mine and Brandon was not having it and we almost got into a fight because I didn't understand why he would be so against meeting one of my friends. At the end of the second date I broke it off with Brandon, I knew he wasn't the one for me. After I told him this didn't feel right and I walked away I noticed him across the street from me, pacing... Back and forth. And I felt guilty so I took him back.

Brandon and I were together for five and a half Miserable years. It was over for me summer of 2012 at that time I was working for a Market Research Firm Monday-Friday 8-5. It was a 2 hour trip to and from work and at that time I was using Public Transportation. By the time I got home I was too tired to engage in sexual activities I would usually eat and go to bed.

One time I woke up in the middle of the night around 1-2am I immediately used the restroom and found out that I had been penetrated in my sleep by Brandon! I was furious and in physical pain. The next morning I had to make a decision. Do I go to work and pretend everything is okay or do I go to the hospital? Being a Special Victims Fan at the time I decided to get proof IF i was going to turn him in. I talked to Brandon on Facebook and played stupid asking him what happened the night before. I got a full confession on

Facebook. But since my world revolved around him and his family I didn't have anyone telling me what the right thing to do was. So I went to work and pretended nothing had happened. When his mother picked me up from work I told her what happened and she told me it wasn't rape. So I thought I was over reacting. But of course she isn't going to admit that her own son could do such a thing and admit to any of his wrong doings.

Besides this could have meant jail time for him! After the sexual assault took place then came the physical abuse on his end. I remember one time Summer of 2014 at a Public Bus Stop he had slapped me, I remember a strange woman yelled from her vehicle to us/him that he had better stop it. A month later we had gotten into another heated argument over some stupid family drama and again he slapped me.

April 2015 God Sent me an Angel, his name is Barton Hogeland, I also met him online on the website "Plenty of Fish" I told him about the abuse I was going thru with Brandon and he was there for me when no one else was. We started talking online every day all day long. He would tell me that I could contact him at anytime day or night and he would be there for me. Brandon tried really hard coming in between us but for me it was clear what I had to do.

May 1st 2015 I moved away with Barton to The Oregon Coast and I have never been this happy! on May 1st Barton had been driving all that week to drive from Salem to Portland until I was comfortable enough to go and live with him and escape the abuse from Brandon. The day I left in May Brandon ended up getting a 2X4 and was threatening Barton and I. Barton had to quickly come pick me up and I had to take a bag of clothes and my 2 dogs and make a run for it.

That was 8 months ago and I haven't looked back! And even though I have lost everything. All my clothes, family belongings, ect. But I have gained way more than I have lost.

👑 **Survivor: Kendall**

*   *   *

I met my abuser in March of 1989
and in April of that year my mother had
terminal cancer, that was hard for me
to take. He was always there but I
didn't see him much except for the
weekends. I worked and when I didn't

work I was helping my mom. She
worked up until August of that year,
and then she had to stop working. I
decided that I was going to stay home
with her and take her to appointments.

He was about 9 years older than me
and had been married before, and had a
2 year old at the time. As the time went
on my mother passed and he was there,
my family didn't like him to much they
kept telling me there is something odd
about him just be careful. In February
of 1990 we eloped and went to SC and
got married. It took me a few months
to tell my brothers and my dad we had
got married, In Aug of that year I got a
call that my dad was on his way to
Duke by helicopter due to a major
heart attack

. I spent a lot of time with my dad
and my family at the hospital. I think

that was when the abuse started ,verbal and mental abuse started then the broken noses and black eyes come. I believe it was because I was with my family and not with him . I always made excuses on why I had a black eye or why my nose got broke. It broke my dad's heart. and he passed away.

I let the abuse go on for several years thinking he would be the same person i fell in love with. I was getting really tired of the bruises and name calling. when I did try to leave he would threaten my family. One Friday afternoon I wanted to go visit my family, This enraged him so . I ended up staying the whole weekend and when I went back home he was so mad with me, His daughter (now 5) was visiting for the summer. I had got up and went to the bathroom and came out and started playing with her. He started screaming "If you two bitches don't stop I'm going to take off my belt and beat the both of you" I laughed a little and he got up, took off his belt and started hitting me with it, my legs and arms, tried to turn me over and get my back but he stopped when his daughter started screaming for him to stop.

I called my sister-in- law and told her what happened. I got what I could and got into my car and left to my friends house. My brother and sister-in-law came and took me to the police station. They told them to take me to hospital they STOPPED counting at 40 bruises on just one leg

Then with all this happening I found out from his ex-wife he use to beat her too. When she didn't do what he wanted her to do. He was arrested and had to spend 90 days in jail and had to do a 12 step anger management program then was let out jail early.

I went to counseling for a few weeks and that helped me realize it wasn't my fault it made me learn a lot about myself. it's been a few years but when I think about what happened it still upsets me. Its painful when you think someone that is supposed to love you and then they want to try and control what you do, where you go, when you talk to your friends or see your family. This is not love. This is abuse.

👑 Survivor: Laurie

*   *   *

My abuser came along through the Internet. I was on line one night with no intentions of finding love at all. I had just broken up with my first boyfriend and I came across this good looking, sweet, short Hispanic man with great lips and smile. So I messaged him to get some information about him. What harm would be done I was thinking.

We seem to hit it off very well. Days go by and he asks me if I would like to catch a movie. I freak out because I have never done this before. I agree to go and arriving at the movies I see this short 4'9 man who looks so cute at the front door and I am smitten fast. We watch the movie and two hours later we are sitting outside talking and getting to know each other. He kept complimenting me on my lips. Flattered to get a compliment like that. He was a gentleman the first date.

Days go by and he is blowing up my phone telling me how sexy I was and what would I do if he asked to see me every day. I found that funny. Why would someone want to see me every day? He asks me out again and on this date he spends a lot of time resting. The second date he mentions he has been married before and has three girls and he is going into the military. I am thinking I don't have a long time to get to know him so I will just enjoy what time I have. As he walks me to my car that night he leans up to kiss me. I got a warm feeling inside and I leave smiling.

The next day I am invited over to his house to meet his family and kids. His brothers are wonderful. The kids were shy. We sit and play video games. We go into his room and chat. Then we make out as well. And one thing lead to the next. I got the pleasure of escorting him to the hotel to check in to leave for boot camp. As well as taking him there, I end up meeting the ex wife. Let me tell you the looks I got from her I would surely be dead.

My feelings for this guy were so strong nothing or any ones looks would stop me from being with him. The three months he was gone I somehow became a part of his kids life as well as ex wife. She managed to get my number from him. I didn't approve.

The stories this lady told me about him were horrible. She told me he disappeared every time she had went into labor for months at a time. And he invited random girls to their wedding, he was saying other women names during sex, That he hit her. I was hurt inside because I was feeling so strong for him.

The only way to keep in touch is by letter. I receive one letter asking me to marry him. I had the biggest smile on my face . I respond asking if he was serious. He writes he loves me so much he has never felt this way about anyone before. Not even his ex. He wrote me with a date and where to get the license.

The time comes for him to come home, and the kids and I go to pick him up at the airport. He just looks at me with love in his eyes. With the date he set to marry coming two days from then. I start talking about the wedding I have always wanted. He stops me and says he doesn't have time for a big wedding. He needed to be reporting to his station in a week. Getting his wish we do the court wedding. My mother is nice enough to plan a reception with my church.

After we get married problems start with his ex. She was scaring us and saying the girls weren't happy about it. Funny they couldn't talk about it.

They actually got to sign on as witnesses on the certificate. Happily married (at the time) we don't do a honeymoon . He didn't understand why we needed one.

The day of the reception comes and we are leaving that night to Washington where he was stationed. For someone who just got married he didn't seem real happy. We got there and not everyone was there. Everyone in my family had some issues with him right away. He kept his eye on one particular guest. I wanted to dance with him and he didn't. Gift time came and the kids were outside playing and ran to get their dad saying mommy is outside. I am furious. I told her she is not welcome. So he jumps and goes outside well I look like fool alone opening the gifts. Coming back minutes later he says sorry and kisses me. I am having this gut feeling this lady is going to be a big problem.

The bossiness starts as we go home to pack for our trip. He is sitting on his behind and telling me it's my job to pack his things. Well I try to pack mine. Everything I packed he asked why I was taking that or did I need that. Me being a Christian, I was told to never question what your husband asks of you and you need to be a submissive wife always. So I leave everything of mine behind. Only having my clothes and Jeep. Not feeling too excited to leave my great job, friends or family. I head on my way to Washington to start my life as a military wife. We get there with just our suitcase we left with.

The first week there we lived in a hotel. He was so mad at me for leaving my jeep behind. Being in a new climate

I was always sick. I had these crazy
spots all over my body that wouldn't go
away. He said I needed to do
something about that. What was I to
do. I thank God for his Sgt. Helping us
find a place and giving us a loan. He
didn't get paid right away. It was hard
and not planned. We could have
planned it better. I suggested he comes
to find a place then send for me. Nope
it had to be what he said.

We go back to get the jeep back
home. Only allowed three days off and
reporting back four days from then.
First thing he wants to do back home
is go to the gym. After the gym he
ends up meeting with his ex. Giving
her all our new information in
Washington. Even how much money
he will be making. The thought of
being a good wife I keep my mouth
shut.

When his visit with her is done he goes to his brother's home, where we are staying and talks all about the females he seen at the gym and how sexy they are. We get a ride to my parents to get my jeep. I wanted to stay and visit with them, but he stays in the car and tells me to just get my keys. That we have things to do. I had every right to visit my family thinking back, but I obeyed.

Once the trip was over we went to base and speak to housing. Thank you Jesus we found a place.

We moved into our place. I am trying to make it a home for my husband. Doing all the things a wife is to do. Wash his uniforms. Iron them for him. Put his special pins on his shirt. Boots shiny and cleaned. Every day I do all I can do with what little we had. We had a few things he found by the trash. I always cooked for him with what food we had. My uncle and aunt gave us some food. Two boxes of it. I am forever thankful. One night he came home and tells me he doesn't like American food. He is the beans, potatoes, meat and tortilla kind of man. Telling me next time buy those things he can eat. Frustrated I start to cry, how can I buy those you don't give me money to do so or even let me have my car to do so. So he leaves after I cooked and goes and gets some tacos from those buses that sell food. Without picking a fight I just put the food away and wash his uniform.

Three hours pass and he isn't back. He enters the door and I look at him angry he tells me he decided to sign up for the gym. Every time I asked for a few bucks he doesn't have money.

Once again he starts talking about all the beautiful women in Washington and how big their behinds are. As usual I am laughing it off.

All this strange stuff going on I have no one to talk to. I remembered I have my Aunt and Uncle here my mom told me I can talk to them. When my uncle brought me the food boxes he said his Daughter in law knows a lot of things about military stuff and things the wives should know. He would give her my number. I had some relief, only because that meant I was going to make a friend and that I really needed it at this point.

Big surprise, He doesn't like the fact that now I have a friend. I have gotten to the point of doing whatever I can do make him happy. A few days goes by

and I don't speak to my new friend
only because he didn't like the fact my
attention was elsewhere. He was
always wanting the attention all on him.
That is what it was suppose to be now.

His phone is starting to go off at
night time now. More like early
morning hours. I just go back to sleep
until it's time for him to get up. Part of
me wanted to go check his phone.
Honestly who in the world sends text
messages at 3 am.? An hour goes by
and he gets up to go to the shower and
it's a perfect chance to get his phone.
There it is plain as day text messages
from some girl in our town. My first
thoughts were not anger, it was how
can he have time to meet anyone here.
We have only been in Washington a
month and half. He works then goes to
the gym then home to shower and relax
before bed. After finding the messages

that morning he goes to the gym after work and my brain was also telling me to check his laptop too.

This man is not the brightest crayon. He never clears his history on the laptop. I took a peek and the last site was a dating site to meet locals in your town. As I enter the site noticing he didn't sign off. Almost like he wants to get found out. Lots of women on there and tons of messages. I click on a new one and I read it. My husband had a thing for bigger curvier women not toothpick skinny.

This girl who sent a new message to him that morning around the same time his phone went off. She was telling him she couldn't meet him at the gym. Well there is the answer I was looking for on how he even had time to meet anyone.

My next move is to send this lady a
message back telling her to leave my
husband alone. The message back was
a nice one. The lady sends an email
back saying she was real sorry and she
had no idea he was married. His profile
said he was single. No surprise there.
She tells me he is a pig and she will
never speak to him again.

He never actually acknowledged the
idea of being married. I was beginning
to feel I was just a convenience to him
just so he can get more money from the
military for being married. Sure wasn't
feeling like a wife the way he was with
me.

His antics are starting to get worse
as the days go by. Which means I am
falling out of love with him.

He starts to force himself on me sexually the wrong awful way. Causing me pain it hurts so bad. I tell him it hurts and to please stop. No he is still going. He obviously didn't care as long as he got his jollies off. After he is finished I am showering to clean my body off. I cry and cry, praying to God, what did I do to deserve this. I had a feeling in my heart that being a submissive wife doesn't mean going through this abuse. It hurt. Inside and out.

Days go by and I am in so much pain, to what I thought was back pain due to sleeping on the concrete floor for so long. He never felt it was important to have a bed. So I ask him if he can take me to the hospital. Biting my head off he tells me to walk there. My feelings are yet hurt again. This fool really doesn't care about me. I am crying begging him to go with me he says he can't keep up with me, I am always sick. So I grab my keys and get in my car and take myself. In the emergency room for twelve hours.

All I think about is getting out of there in time to get the car back so he can report to work. The doctor comes in and tells me I need surgery in the rectum. I have my cell and I call my parents back home. They are worried not being able to be with me. Night time after visiting hours he shows up. Not in his uniform but fancy new clothes with a new phone with cologne on. Well I am having surgery he is out shopping with the money he never has and new clothes. This man. I tell him to leave. So he asks the nurse when am I going to be released. The next day is what he was told. So he says good night and told me I better be in a better mood tomorrow.

After being home I fall into this deep depression. I am miserable here and I have no one. I am one to want to be verbal and talk things out. Every time I try to speak to him he always brings up divorce, or how I'm just like his ex wife. I go to the living room and open my bible to read. It always calms me. Every time he seen me reading my bible he would shake his head and laugh.

One time we were having intercourse having his lifeline(his cell) and he was really into, which is rare. He goes to the bathroom when finish and his phone is above my head. I look and I am curious to what has his attention so much, he wasn't looking at me. I turn it on. There is a picture of a guest from our reception. He was in love with her. It is time this fool gets his payback. Why isn't he attracted to me? I do everything for him. The next day he gets in trouble by his Sgt. because of me and that's when he tries to hit me. Catching me on a bad day I finally tell him off. If you hit me make it good because I have so much anger I will kick your little A--. So he stops.

Weeks later we get word he is released and we are going home. Thrilled as ever I can't wait to go home to leave him. Now I can stop trying to find ways to escape. God opened a chance for me. We're released now and trying to pack the little jeep. He has to take all his stuff home for memories. So he throws some of my things out so his stuff can fit.

It was a peaceful trip home. We are back home and I been busting butt doing school. He got a job and took my car everywhere. That way he knew I was home. He was always late picking me up from my parents, where I did school. Remembering one time my back seats were down and the jeep smelled like women's perfume. Those seats weren't down when   I was dropped off at four am.

His company had a party and he handpicked a lady for the Christmas party for secret Santa. He asks me to get a Victoria secrets gift card for a co worker. I try to get invited to the company party. He makes every excuse in the book for me not to go.

Valentine's day is here and I finally have my car to go get some things for the house. I put the things In the back and I find a receipt for a dozen roses, a teddy, and a card. Not for me. I didn't get anything. So being to the point I cry all the time for sadness and anger. In even got called pathetic because I am always crying.

Three nights after Valentine's day he rapes me yet again. Not once but twice. After I had surgery it's not the same for me back there. I am crying and screaming again. He doesn't stop. I am feeling this is my fault. Each time I was raped I was always praying to God to just give me strength to continue to be that submissive wife.

My friends mom takes me to the hospital and guess what?? I got more abscesses to be removed. They were external this time. I am escorted to a room in the emergency room where two student doctors tell me they will be doing my surgery. Kind of scared. They were saying they have never done it yet. Giving me an injection to numb they start to do the surgery. I feel EVERYTHING. I AM DONE

! I am on a mission to get this abuse out of my life. It's gotten to the point I sleep sideways on bed so he doesn't touch me. Crying myself to sleep every night still continuing praying to God. That weekend comes and the deal was I can have my car and do things. Well that's what I told him was going to happen. The hard part was getting my keys from him. I find out from his girls that their dad is hanging out with this chick from work with them In tow.

Next day he gets his income taxes back, And I visited my mom that day. When I get back he takes my wrist and takes me into the room and asks me to look around and see what is missing. I am looking all around. He calls me all these names, including comparing me to his ex. Finally I tell him to shut up and tell me something already. So he says nothing. Then I went off on him. Got in his face and told him he is a jerk, rude selfish man who only thinks of himself. He tells me he doesn't need my ass or my car. THANK YOU JESUS. That's my sign. Get my sandals on, grab my keys and purse and I am out of there. Of course crying. I took my vows seriously for that year but it's hard being the only one loving the other.

I head to my parents and cry and cry. Taking my rings off. Staying the night there. Half way through the night I get a text from him asking me when I am coming home. and that he never said all those nasty things to me.

I was so hurt but relieved. Domestic abuse is the worse things anyone can experience. It messes with your self esteem and your trust. It has been three years and I have started to move on and believe I am worth something more than my past, and I am waiting for God to bring that special man I deserve my way. The one who knows how to treat a woman and will treat me the way I deserve.

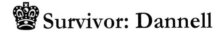 **Survivor: Dannell**

AMBERLEE HOAGLAND

* * *

Mother Fu*ker

She lives in denial, prefers to forget,
Than admit the truth that she may
regret,
 Of how she treated me so cruel,
 For everything she had a rule

My confidence she shattered,
 Flesh and bones she battered,
 Shout, snarl and spit,
 Refer to me as 'It'

I would clean the house from top to
bottom,
She would search for something I had
forgotten,
Argue with my Father, off he would
storm,
She would take it out on me for being
born

For friends and family she would act so
fake,
  Invite people over happily passing
round cake,
  I knew I was safe if only for a while,

And she was still watching through
her smile

I found a few things to do in the day
Imagine I was somewhere far far away,
Music and books plus a strong
imagination
Would for a while block the
aggravation

I would think this fat beast cannot be
my Mum,
And there would be a day my real Mum
would come,
This Mum only wanted the lost son
that she mourned,
'If I only I was a boy' I was daily
informed

A mad frenzy of punches, kicks, chunks
of hair,
Beat me with an ironing board wet t-
towels, a chair,
Her explanation for my bruises was not
a surprise,
The school was told I was a tom boy
who also tells lies

Locked in my room with no food for
days on end,
As I was an embarrassment to her
family and friend,
 I was never allowed to cry, be in pain
or feel unwell,
That was what I deserved for being an
evil girl

At 15 I hit back what did I have to
lose,
She had used nearly every kind of
abuse,
 I have never told my dad he would just
say No way!,

It has never been mentioned to this
very day
We will never be close and she still has
her say,
I don't argue back, I just smile thinking
each day,
You may think you beat me but you
have not won,

Because I have a loving daughter,
where's your loving son!

🜲 **Survivor: Tear Phonix**

*   *   *

Sinister Smile

Flashes of sinister smiles, whispers of
secrets kept
Loss of young innocence, tears that
were never wept
'I'll teach you some things' he leers 'I
see what you are'

He licks his lips as he rasps 'boys like
girls who go far'
His eyes strip my body, as he excitedly
shuffles about
Breathing heavily, what's on his mind
there is no doubt
Acting shifty, sweat on his brow, his
face flushed red
He says I'm provocative then tells me
to sit on the bed
In walks a boy, his head bowed down,
he's about my age
'You and my grandson are going to do
a play the bed is the stage'
That's when things fade become a blur
but I remember this much
We have to do things with body parts
that we don't want to touch

The sound of his panting, the sight of
his thing swollen in his hand
He has full power, total satisfaction this
is just how he had planned
For three years this went on the three
of us or just us two
But it was always him that decided what
he wanted me to do
'Its your fault, it's what men will expect
from your type of girl'
'This is our special secret, I'll buy some
sweets if you don't tell'
The adults never suspected they
wouldn't even think twice
They just saw an old man who was
always friendly and nice
He would even look different,
softening his face and smile

It was only his grandson and me that could see the pedophile.

👑 **Survivor: Tear Phonix**

* * *

Demons

Have you met your demon? Believe me
they are there
Patiently waiting in the shadows of
your souls lair
I hope for your sake you have only one
For no fear is worse than forgetting
what was done

Don't keep things suppressed you have
to deal now
I know how it hurts but you have to get
them out somehow

The deeper they lurk the more they rot
your brain
Tricking your senses until they drive
you insane
They never let you rest even sleep is no
escape
Paralyzed as you see them repeat the
beatings and rape
Feed you drops of evil that sicken your
insides
Follow you as they whisper, tattoo you
with their eyes

In the end you believe they are as real
as me and you
Please consider my words, do you want
to be haunted to?

Reflection

I look in the mirror, what do I see
A person that I wish was not me
I look deeply in to my eyes
Sadness there I cant disguise
Where did the girl I used to see go
The answer to that I really don't know
If I smash the mirror will I find
The pieces of me I left behind
Could I pick up a shard to cut away
The chains that hold me back each day
I am not looking for perfection
Just to be happy with my reflection!

Survivor: Tear Phonix

*　　*　　*

In 2004 I met my ex-
husband/abuser in the UK (he is white
South African) when I was 28. We
dated for a little while and lived
together after about only 4 months.
When he told me that he was coming
back to South Africa to live, he asked
me to come and move to South Africa
with him. At this point he was a
completely different person, very nice
to me and not abusive at all. Up to this
point I have never been a victim of

physical domestic violence or abuse before as an adult.

I was no stranger to abuse however. My whole life I was told by my family what a terrible person I am, how I was fat, ugly, useless, stupid and because of these things no boy or man would ever want me or to date me, that I would be single always and do nothing with my life.

I would be constantly screamed at for everything and criticized about every little thing. I was often threatened by my father if I should tell anyone about this abuse, I would be beaten into next week and that no one would ever believe me. I was never frightened and never got hit but many threats. As I knew this was not true of me, although I have often felt ugly my whole life.

I knew I was smart – went to
rubbish schools but had a high IQ and
my friends always liked me. I decided
to leave home as soon as possible. I
worked hard got top grades and applied
to University to do A levels and Law
Degree. Even when I graduated with a
first, this was never good enough for
my family. I never received any praise
or thanks for anything.

When I look back on the last 11
years I have known my ex even when
he was nice with me in the beginning. I
could even see a few things now,
looking back on it. He used to make
snide remarks about my appearance like
he thought I was too big, too fat,
overweight, too tall

We started arguing more and more
after I moved to South Africa with him

and by the time it was clear I was
trapped with no money, no income, not
able to work, no car (isolated and
imprisoned really) he changed quickly
now he had me where he wanted me.

I was so upset that he had changed
and been lied to for months. He started
putting me down constantly that I was
not allowed to think for myself, say
anything, and answer back. The house
was never clean enough or tidy enough
as I didn't clean the house 5 days a
week like the South African white way
with a maid, and never had a maid, as a
Brit and to most people, this isn't
normal. I had to do everything for him
and myself (which honestly I have
always done for myself since a young
age) – cleaning, cooking, washing,
washing up. It got so bad living with
little money – no washing machine had
to hand wash a lot, and painstakingly

sweeping the carpet with a brush with
no Hoover. The sicker I got the more I
struggle to clean the house and look
after kids. I very rarely had a Hoover
and no washing machine for years, very
little furniture, had to sit on the floor
for years and no table a lot of the time,
and worsened my arthritis.

I was only allowed to go to the
shops once a week, where I would have
to go to vile shops with cash and got
screamed at in the car. I had to be
there a certain amount of time and
would go berserk if I was there too
long or too short a time, without a
doubt the most impatient person
possible. In my case I am in the most
abusive country on earth, where it is
always legal to abuse women, In fact
South African men are the most
abusive men in the world. Women have
so few little rights and generally go with

the attitude that abuse is always normal and so legal. It is impossible to press charges against men over assault or domestic violence. South Africa has the highest statistics - 1 woman in this country is killed by an abusive partner/spouse every 6 hours. It also has the highest level of rape of about 1400 women are raped in this country every day.

Even after a highly publicized case of Oscar Pretorius for murdering his girlfriend - they will never overturn the law to protect women. I am also a lawyer but am not legally allowed to work over here as a foreign national.

My other problem with being in South Africa has always been not being in my own country and I had no idea how hellish South African men are and how utterly awful, hellish South Africa would be. My ex husband lied to me about so many things including that I would be able to work over here. So instead I found myself in a country where I was purposely isolated, always alone, couldn't work, couldn't even get a bank account and no public transport, had no friends, no life of my own.

He was so controlling with me that I was not allowed any life of my own and couldn't go anywhere alone as I was never allowed a car. Never had I regretted it so much but when I asked to leave over and over again and go home to my country as I only ever have temporary residency over here as South African immigration is so severe I was never allowed to be a resident and I have been subjected to so much racism always as a foreign national and for the color of my skin.

Very early on after moving to this country my ex-husband starts becoming emotionally abusive and financially controlling. With his emotional abuse he was so belittling with me about everything, he would blame me for everything and criticize every little about me and my life.

What made it worse was that I had lost my whole life and was isolated on purpose and we were living with his mother and stepfather in their house in Pretoria. His whole family is very abusive and racist people, and always made racist remarks. They were always so verbally abusive with me and wouldn't let me use the net or the landline in their house. I used to go to internet cafes as this was the only contact I had with the outside world.

Living with my abusers parents was
so hellish with me and they constantly
made threats. I was basically asked to
leave their house as I wouldn't
apologize for arguing with his
stepfather on one occasion and moved
into a studio flat in Johannesburg. And
yet still I was not allowed to go home.
At this point my ex started following
me about the flat and when arguing
with me - he would literally put me in a
corner in a room and block the door
off so I couldn't get out of the room
and would scream at me. He wasn't
always around and kept making excuses
as to why he wouldn't come back to the
flat at night. I later found out he was
having an affair.

I thought at this point it was because
of his drug addictions. He had been
very clever at hiding his drug use up to
this point but suddenly his personal

hygiene went downhill very fast by him only having a bath once a week. He became a totally revolting, crazy and evil addict. There was never any money as he would happily spend all of his money on drugs and takeaways and make sure I was poor and hungry. All of this continued for years. At this point, I really saw his violent temper - especially when I asked him to at least stop smoking in the bathroom. He got so violent - that he went about the flat - kicking and punching the walls, the furniture all the doors and broke off the toilet seat in a violent rage. More and more over time he would stamp about, slam doors and violently smack crockery down on surfaces, endless violent rages.

He then started ripping up books, burning them and throwing my possessions on bonfires in the garden and burning everything. If this wasn't bad enough he would also throw plates, bowls, glasses and cups at the wall and break everything and then after the first beating, he would throw crockery at me. He never replaced anything and I was constantly blamed for everything. And I always asked to go home but always got told "you are not going anyway and I didn't deserve a life of my own". Never seen anyone more evil in my life.

About a year after this - he started becoming physically abusive with me. Needless to say it destroyed me and devastated me. The entire level of abuse for so long was so utterly soul destroying. I always remember the first time he punched me. I was standing by a swimming pool in Johannesburg and we were arguing and the next thing I know I got punched several times in the face. I was in so much shock and in so much pain, I did nothing other than scream and cry and had the shock of bruises on my face.

I knew this wouldn't be the last time but I never thought it would happen to me. 6 weeks or so after that I got a severe beating in the house for daring to argue back. This time he never hit my face and basically never has hit my face since then. This time I hit and kicked back which antagonized him further and got my left arm dislocated and kicked further why he dared scream at me that I should never defend myself. I went to the police station with many bruises and injuries and got laughed at and told "This is South Africa and you are a foreign national and its legal here"

The emotional and physical abuse
never ended and went on for 10 years
for me in South Africa. I would fight
back in the beginning against his
physical abuse as I am not the sort of
person to be punched and kicked but
he was stronger than me, and would get
angrier for this and would often
dislocate my left arm and kick my bad
left leg back that I would be on the
floor in screaming pain and would be
kicked and punched more. I would
often be covered in bruises and injuries.
He would often punch and kick me all
over, dig his nails into my skin, pull my
hair, smack my head against the wall
and shake my body. Then there were
times when he would throw heavy
groceries at me and slam a door in my
face on purpose.

I tried the police yet again in another
state of KZN (the first time I went to

the police was in Gauteng). Exactly the same story. By the time I became pregnant - I could no longer defend myself. I nearly miscarried my children as he would abuse me physically when I was pregnant too.

The worst came for me in 2010 when he had been asking me for money for days – although I rarely had any of my own, to mostly buy drugs. I refused and we had a huge argument and started telling me that I was such a bitch and that I didn't deserve to live and that I wasn't going anywhere. "you don't deserve to live" and threw me hard against the wall and started smacking my head very hard against the wall and soon put his hands around my neck and started to strangle me.

Many thoughts went through my mind at the time – mostly for my 2 year old daughter and what would she do without me. I honestly thought I was going to die and after everything that this was the way I would die. I had been screaming for help and was too weak to fight as I was on chemotherapy at the time, I lost my voice and consciousness. The whole time my 2 year old was screaming at him and tried to pull him off me without avail. I remember nothing until I regained consciousness and was on a heap on the floor with my 2 year old little girl sobbing next to me. To this day I will always wonder what that did to her. I was grateful to be alive and after that I always knew that this was the worst he could do to me. Even though I asked for a divorce more and more after this, still always refused one.

When I fell pregnant by accident in 2012 - he kept telling me to have an abortion as he didn't want the baby and that I would be severely punished if I chose to keep her. Which I did but he got even more physically and emotionally abusive with me during this pregnancy. He still blames me for keeping my youngest daughter. For years he had constantly threatened my life by telling me he wants me dead and I don't deserve to live.

All the abuse as well as all the harassment and my ailing health took such a toll on me that I had a stroke in December 2014. After my stroke I was hospitalized and endured more racist comments usually that as a white foreign national I shouldn't be in their black hospital. After being brutally harassed and slandered, I tried to discharge myself 2 days before Christmas in December 2013 only for them to refuse to drag me down a

corridor by 7 black men and be locked
into a hospital room which held 13
black nurses (including 5 men and 2
male security guards). Whom threw me
onto a bed held me down and had 5
men beat me for 40 minutes within an
inch of my life. The worst beating of
my life.

They put their hands hard over my
mouth and put their hands around my
neck and strangled me. I was terrified
and am still haunted by this. I thought I
would die they laughed and made
nothing but racist remarks all 13 of
them including women.

They tried to kill me but my ex came
into the hospital and they dragged me
off the bed tied me with rope to a chair
bound my feet and hands and my kids
saw me like this, dripping in blood.
They reluctantly untied me and was

eventually discharged. My ex was so vile to me about this also and he reluctantly agreed to a divorce after this. Although it has taken 15 months to get on with divorce proceedings. I am amazed I am still alive.

It is hard for me to still have to see my ex-husband a lot because of my kids but at least I am free of domestic violence.

In normal circumstances you would call the police who would arrest your spouse/partner and charge him and ask for a protection order. Whilst your partner/spouse has been charged and usually gets tried in court and will get a sentence. This is what you normally do when you are outside of South Africa. Instead I had to survive domestic violence.

I can see why from my own experiences why women get killed from abuse. Although I have gotten injuries from this and been greatly traumatized. But at least there is life after domestic violence.

I hope by telling my story this will help someone. I will always wish to go home to the UK and wish one day my kids and I will finally be home.

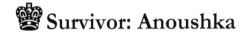 **Survivor: Anoushka**

So here I am. An 'abuse' survivor.
When people say 'abuse' it conjures
images & reenactments of disturbing
popular movies I've seen. They all have
a context, relevant dialogue that all
makes sense as to why somebody may
behave so badly, they have a purposeful
& 'life lesson learned' ending. But that's
not my story. That's not my experience.
That's not my abuse.

I never knew the cycle of abuse started for me pre-birth. I'm an 'intergenerational' victim. My Mother is emotionally void & instilled in me the greatest sense of people-pleasing she possibly could. My Father gave me wonderful gifts of believing I am unworthy of anything good, I must be submissive at all times to a patriarchal society and, above all, I must not talk back. I must never have a voice unless I am saying 'please' or 'thank-you' or more importantly, 'sorry.'

There were times of trouble during my childhood when I wasn't silent when the news was on, or on Saturday morning I was a bit too loud, or even times of not being thankful for the church I was supposed to be controlled by and the men sexually abusing me within it.

As time passed it was ingrained in me to just keep silent and put up with what you get. Which i did, and landed myself a husband that enjoyed making my life hell. Not only did he bruise me with TV remotes, his shoes (gee, he loved throwing those things!) One time a hair gel container... anything in his reach really. But he also specialized in the 'words' that all abusers use....
"you're just lucky I'm here. nobody else would stay around"; "you should be grateful I tell you how to improve yourself"; "nobody will ever love you as much as I do"; "you're a liar- that never happened"; "you've got a bloody good imagination... always making things up"; "well if you didn't do that I wouldn't have reacted like that"; "it's because of you that I act like this.. you make me so mad".

I also endured the relentless hawk's eye... I couldn't go to the toilet without him saying "where are you going"; the phone rings "who is it?.... okay you can talk to your sister but only for 5 minutes, but she's not coming over".

I also had the relentless task of oral stimulation & hideously painful 3 minute penetration to relieve this man of his 'natural urges' and always being told "it doesn't matter where I get my appetite- as long as I eat at home" at the end.

Domestic violence doesn't make sense. It can be small and quiet. It can be a look, a deep sigh, a turn of the head, it can be loud smashing noises, booming voices, fists thrown, heads bashed. I finally left his grasp when he punched me in the middle of a city street when I revealed the news that I was having our second child, a girl. I was 4 months already..... he physically hurt me so deliberately to end this pregnancy and he walked away when he was satisfied he had completed his mission. He left me in the street, empty..... emptied.

I still have to see him on sporadic times because he threatens legal action if I don't permit access to our first child. These are small amounts of supervised times in public places in which he still argues with me about how crazy I am, how unfair I am being, how unwarranted it is to supervise him because he would never hurt our son- it was me that was the problem in our marriage.

I've been to the police, I've been to healing centers, I've secured

ADVO's, I've been to psychologists, I know the language, I know the literature, I know the process of the cycle of DV.
I too can say the words that I believe in love, I believe that one day I might find somebody worthy that treats me well and will help me heal small pieces of my soul.

But at the moment, it's all words.

I want my daughter. I wanted a good husband & partner in life. I didn't want to be hit. I don't want to shudder if there is a loud bang in a shopping mall; I don't want to feel scared if my voice is too loud or I laugh out loud and people might hear me. I don't want my memories to be 'oh that's the place he hit me one time because...' or, ' he killed my baby there....'

Nobody has ever looked at me and told me they know me and love me, every part of me, and I'm not in trouble for any part of it.

I want new words in my life. Words that mean something real to me. I don't want to hear "one day he'll get what's coming to him" or "that's sad... you're so brave. have you found a new love in your life yet? you have to move on and stop living in the past", "why did you stay with him? I would have left the second he did anything".

I am so damaged from these events. I am so broken from these events. I am so much stronger from these events. But why is everybody talking at me? Words..... just words. When will they mean something? When will they help me feel valued & loved?

To me, that's domestic Violence.... It hasn't ended just because I suddenly understand the words. It's an everyday survival.

Survivor: Sophie

*　　*　　*

Not more than two years ago, I escaped an abusive marriage. I flew over the miles to find peace, refuge and security. It is by far the bravest thing I have done, besides not giving up on life in the midst of the turmoil of the unrelenting darkness that surrounded me all those years. Growing up in an environment where abuse was seen as a norm, I pushed away the warning signs that this relationship was no good for me. In fact, I blamed myself and thought I deserved to be treated badly; to be punished for my mistakes. Most often, I shut out the still small voice in my heart that yearned to bring me comfort in saying that I was not alone.

To deal with the pain of abuse and rejection, I turned into an addict of sorts. It seemed like this was my only escape from reality. It was the only way to ease the pain of emotional hurt, negligence and crazy games. For me, it seemed like the only way to survive and get through another night. Kept away from the counsel of my family and friends, I had no one I could freely open to with the assurance of receiving help. I woke up each day with a sense of fear from the nightmares that stole my sleep almost each night. Sitting in fear all day of what would happen next, I could hardly ever eat. Even more, I withdrew from people, kept to myself and drowned in a deep sea of depression accompanied most often by fantasies of death.

A month after my second attempt to kill myself, I met two wonderful people who became life-changing friends. With their help, I was able to get away from the abuse and danger and I soon found solace in a Non-Profit in New Delhi, India. I was lucky to find them since the support they have given me is beyond what they even promise to do. Today, not only do I have their help as a domestic violence survivor but am also given the opportunity to creatively be part of the work they do in bringing care and support to those in need.

I still struggle with depression and pangs of anxiety each time I am in a new situation that I was never allowed to experience before. However, with support from new friends, community and God, I am able to overcome. It was never easy being in the trauma of abuse, feeling like my heart weighed so much so that I couldn't even find the strength to get out of bed and put my feet on the floor. But even now that I am far from such pain, it still isn't easy cause my mind is so used to believing that there is always something to be afraid or hyper vigilant about. It is still so easy to think that nothing is ever going to be okay after all that has happened.

However, today I choose to believe differently. With help and hard work life is hopeful. I urge you today to be that friend who believes in the story of the one who needs you to count on. Perhaps, if you don't know what to do, find someone who does. And if you are the one hiding behind the pain of fear and abuse today, I urge you to never give up because help is possible.

The movement begins with you and me.

 **Survivor: Annah**

As best I can remember, the abuse started when I was around 5. My memories are still very unreliable, I believe that's common in people with Post Traumatic Stress Disorder. I didn't fit in at school, because I grew up dirt poor, so the kids who lived next door to my grandmother were all I had to play with. I stayed at my granny's house often because my parents both worked overtime.

She had two jobs as well, so I was often sent to the neighbors during the day. They had a lot of kids, I don't really remember how many. My little brother didn't have to go because he was in an after school program. It started out fairly innocently. They had a son around my age and one a few years older. There was a shed in their backyard that we converted into our clubhouse. We defended it against invading forces, sailed it to deserted islands in search of buried treasure, flew it to mars, and held clandestine meetings in deep subterranean chambers beneath it. For the younger brother Alex and I, though, it eventually became Hell on Earth. The older brother, Mark, was the "boss" of our club. He decided where the ship sailed and what planets we flew to. We had to do what he said, otherwise there was beatings for insubordination.

Sometimes we had to take off our clothes. If we were injured in battle, we had to go to the doctor. If we required space suits, we had to change. It wasn't a big deal at first. Some examinations required that he masturbate us. Eventually sexual activity became a major component of our games, but it was mutual and probably harmless at the beginning. One day, however, he penetrated me anally with his finger. I told him to stop because it hurt, but he kept going, insisting I would "die" if he didn't. I told him I didn't want to play anymore, and he became angry. He beat me up and forced me to allow him to continue.

The next day, at some point, he told me in so many words that he was going to have anal sex with me. I told him no because it would hurt. He got angry and laid me out with a single punch. I was dazed and on the concrete floor. He picked me up (he was much larger than I) and bent me over a tractor lawnmower. I felt his hand undo the front of my shorts, and all at once he was inside me. All I remember is that it hurt at first, and then it's like this black cloud descends over my vision and I don't remember anything except telling my mom that I was sick and being sent to my room for the night. I spent the next day home sick from school, sleeping at their house (Gran had to work). He attacked me while I was asleep and raped me in his little brother's bed. His mother walked in on it. She just left and didn't say anything.

My grandmother was no prize herself. She wasn't a horrible person, she genuinely cared for my brother and I and typically would spoil us with presents every now and then. But she was also a very harsh woman. We had hours of chores before and after school, and we frequently took lashings for insolence. I was locked in the basement more than once as a punishment. One time, after being raped next door a few hours before, I was examining myself in my bedroom when my grandmother walked in. She accused me of masturbating and bent me over the bed. When she was really angry, she wouldn't stop hitting you until you stopped crying. I think at some point I just shut down and stopped. My teacher laughed at me the next day when I asked to be allowed to stand during class.

I was also forced to do things with his younger brother; a few times I was even forced to rape him. I think the whole family was tied up in it. I have vague recollections of seeing their father with their younger sister, they were all afraid of him. I try not to dig at the memories, because they're just going to upset me and it's more problems than it's worth.

It went on like that until I was about 12. Around that time, my mother found a new job that allowed her to be home in the mornings and I was judged old enough to be home by myself for a few hours a day. The family moved out of the house when I was 12 or 13 or so. I never saw them again. That was it.

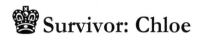 **Survivor: Chloe**

*   *   *

I met my abuser in 2011, after separating from my abusive alcoholic husband of 8 years. When I reflect on the things that I have survived over the past 5 years, I'm beyond proud of myself, but I'm also horrified. There is a lot that I have repressed and I am still working currently through. The healing process isn't for the faint of heart, and there is a recovery process that I have to actively work on daily. As I have been working through this time in my life I am still in shock of what my reality was. I still have strong feelings of embarrassment and shame, but I also feel like a superhero. I survived a man so wicked you would think he was the devil himself.

We met online, which I'm sure is shocking that someone on the internet wouldn't be honest, right? One night my best friend and I got drunk and created a fake profile on some stupid dating website. My profile didn't have a picture, and the bio was just a bunch of ridiculous shenanigans, We were having a blast messing with these guys. It was all just a big joke, but somehow in the process, I ended up liking this guys picture and he sent me a message. We bantered quite well and both of us had a very inappropriate sense of humor. We also bonded over our love of music. I gave him my number and he kept asking me out. I told him I was far too small to make a skin suit out of, but he kept asking me out. His persistence was admirable at the time and eventually I caved. Couldn't hurt, right? Wrong, couldn't have hurt more actually.

When I met my abuser, I was incredibly fragile. I had already been in an abusive relationship (which compared to this one, was a day at the park), and he knew that. I was completely codependent and enabling. I was prey to this man. He took full advantage of my weakness from the very beginning and never stopped. He did it in the most graceful way too, like a waltz he had been doing for years, and I'm sure is continuing with.

We met at a bar, and hit it off immediately. He was smart, charming and had a wonderfully sarcastic sense of humor. There was something devious about him, and he had these big beautiful puppy dog eyes, they got me every time. I remember telling him early on that he could get away with murder, which is now a memory that makes my stomach turn. At the end of our first date he laid a big kiss on me. He was bit awkward but had such confidence, I thought. We continued to talk and hang out and I enjoyed the first couple weeks. I could tell that I made him feel good about himself, which in turn made me feel good. Little did I realize that I was just being used to boost his ego.

If I can ever give any dating advice, it would be to go with your gut. After a couple weeks, red flags started popping up. He stayed distant and I remember being really hurt after we first slept together he didn't call me back the next day. I was so new to dating and naive, so I didn't know if this was a typical thing to do. However, I did notice that he wasn't inviting me over to his house, which seemed peculiar. I called him out on it and jokingly asked if he was hiding me from his wife and kids. He assured me that it was just because his place was a mess or it was because his roommates were annoying.

There was always some excuse and I wanted to get him the benefit of the doubt. However, I am a girl, and naturally began to snoop. I looked him up on facebook and ended up finding out that he did in fact have a girlfriend. I found pictures of them going to the same beach we had just gone to, and the pictures dated back about 2 years. Of course he denied it and said that they were "friends," but it didn't matter anyhow because they were no longer speaking. He continued to tell me that she got really weird and went psycho. In reality, she figured him out and ran. None of his stories ever added up, and I would call him out on, which only angered him, and he became extremely argumentative.

Looking back there were clearly signs of abuse early on, but I just couldn't see it at the time. We would get into fights were I knew I was right, and it was beyond obvious that I was right, but he would somehow turn everything around on me and it was somehow magically my fault. The worst part is that I fell for it every time. He would also play things off like he was kidding to backpedal. I found myself becoming more and more confused as to what really was reality. One night we went on a really amazing, all day adventure. It was a blast and I was exhausted afterwards, and fell asleep in the car. As we got out of his car, I was saying good-bye and that I needed something to keep me awake for my drive home and out of nowhere he slaps me across the face. I'm in absolute shock! I yelled at him and he just started laughing and told me he was just trying to help.

He never apologized for any of his actions or behaviors; he just somehow justified it and would Houdini it into being my fault once again. He slowly began to isolate me. I went to a bar with some of my girlfriends, and a week later I get a text message from some random number. It was a guy that tells me we met at the bar last week and that

I pinched his ass and gave him my number. At first, I thought it was my abuser playing a joke on me, but I responded by saying that I had no recollection of him or that event. We bantered for a minute because I thought the entire thing was bizarre. He described what I looked like, what I was wearing, the girls I was with. He asked if I wanted to meet up with him for a drink, and I denied the offer. I told him that had a boyfriend and I wasn't interested. He kept asking and I just ended the conversation with something along the lines of a "haha maybe." I told my abuser about the random texts and asked if it was him. He said no and began to ask me about the text exchange and demanded to see my phone. He immediately went into a rage and began screaming at me and calling me a liar and a cheater. I began apologizing and trying to explain that I was joking about maybe meeting up. It was obvious that I wasn't going to and I didn't understand why he was mad or how I cheated on him. A year or so later, I get a phone call from that number and it's my abusers friend who said "Hey sorry my phone died and I'm using B's work phone" My heart sank. He set me up.

As the relationship continued, things continued to further spiral out of control. He began to control me sexually. He would make demands of what he wanted and if I said no, he wouldn't let it go and if we came to a compromise or agreement he would then shame me after and tell me I was a whore, slut, cheater, you name it...I was called it. He would also buy me expensive gifts and take me on trips. He held all of those things over my head to keep me controlled. He would tell me that no one would be as good to me as he was, and no one would ever love someone as damaged as me.

I started seeing a therapist, which of course upset him and he wanted to know every detail. I began to tell her about the relationship and she advised me to get out as soon as possible. I mustered up the courage to go to his place and get my belongings which included a photo album of tastefully done, but nude photographs. He saw that I was taking it and he begins to grab my purse from my arm. We begin to fight over my bag, and somehow he grabs a full glass of water throws it in my face and pushes me on the floor while continuing to stand over me and scream at me. He takes the pictures out and throws my bag at me. I pick it up and run out the door which he chases me to and I run into my car but he grabs the door and wedges himself between me and the door. He tells me that I need to be very afraid of him because he is a very scary man, and his family is also full of scary people that won't hesitate to kill me. I threaten to call the cops and he threatens me back.

I panic and call my dad as my abuser is standing over me and staring into my eyes, completely soulless. He almost looks proud of himself. My father tells me to call the cops. I don't remember how I got away, but the next thing I recall is that I'm parked a few blocks away sobbing and I call the police. I filed a report and the cop looked at me and gave me a look I'll never forget. He quietly said to me "I would never do anything like that to my wife." I begged the police not to tell him that I filled the report, but my abuser knew. He told me that he forgave me and that it was all a big misunderstanding and I should stop seeing my therapist. He would tell me that I was his and that I didn't know how to manage my own life and everything would be so much easier if I just let him make all my decisions. To him, I was never a human being, I was a possession. In the beginning he seemed too interested in who I was as a person, my story, my life. I opened up to him about my deepest darkest fears and secrets and he would use them against me.

I met his family and his brothers and friends would occasionally make off-handed comments about him around me. His brother ended up contacting me and told me that I needed to get out of the relationship and that I was being cheated on. I tried to leave him again and again by this point, but now I felt like I had some leverage. This time I tell him I know that he cheated on me, and I was done. He demanded to know where I got my information, and refused to leave me alone. He would call and call.

The harassment was torture, he would not leave me alone until I confessed and I suddenly began to regret even saying that I knew he cheated. He found out it was his brother and he said that he was going to discuss it with his family and that there were a lot of concerns about the mental well-being of his sibling. I believed him, of course. While his brother is telling me all of this information, he is also hitting on me and being completely inappropriate.

After the drama of the situation eases, I'm guilted horribly by my abuser about how I have now ruined the relationship between him and his family. Around this time, he becomes irritated with the relationship I have with my family and is angered when I spend time with them.

One day I had dinner plans with my parents, and he stayed home from work because he was sick. I was lectured for at least 3 hours about what a terrible girlfriend I was and that I shouldn't be spending time with my family, but I be taking care of him instead.

It felt like every day was a new huge fight. I begin to distance myself from him and he showed up at my house. I open the door and refuse to let him in then close the door and lock it. He begins kicking my door repeatedly. I unlock it and swing it open. Now at this time I am living in a really sketchy

neighborhood, but all of my
surrounding neighbors looked out for
one another. I start yelling as loud as I
could for him to get off my property so
they could hear and help me. They
gather outside of my house, then they
tell him to leave. All of a sudden, he
isn't so tough anymore. He gets in his
car and takes off; my neighbor tells me
she sees him drive by a lot.

The back and forth was now very
normal for us. He would have some
reason for blowing up and I would
threaten to leave. He would give me
just enough space to let me calm down
and then weasel his way back in, but I
was the still the one that needed to
change, and he would inform that that
"if you would stop doing this, I
wouldn't have to act that way." I was
beyond drained from constantly being
at war. We end up having a huge fight

over something that I can't recollect, but I remember it ending with my head and a door slamming together and me lying on the bathroom floor curled up in the fetal position crying. I stop talking to him and he continues to try and get me back.

During this break, I got a call from a friend of mine that I had known for about 10 years. He was fighting with his girlfriend, and having difficulty with his father who was an alcoholic. I wanted to be there for him and we went out that night and ended up drinking way too much. We kissed and began to make-out in the backseat of his car. He ended up taking my bottoms off and unzipped his pants. I kept telling him no, and was covering myself up to keep him from entering me. He kept grabbing my hand and pinning it to the side, and after struggling for a bit, he won. After he was finished, he panicked about the time and kicked me out of his car. I stood on the side of the road and called a cab to come get me and take me home. This event has multiple devastations for me. I felt like I couldn't have been more used, and completely disposable. I was so hurt that it was done by someone I trusted, cared for and respected. I felt like my abuser was right when he told me that no one else would want me or love me the way he did.

The craziest part of the relationship with my abuser, was no matter what, he knew when something was wrong. At this point we weren't speaking and I was at a new low after this recent event. It had been a while since we had spoke and out of the blue he sends me a message about how he just wants to hug me. I felt like that connection we had was real, and that he really did love me. When I let him back into my life this time, it was great. He was loving and assured me that things were going to be different this time, but he knew something was wrong. I was acting different, and I didn't want to be intimate. I would cry in the middle of the night, and eventually I opened up and told him that I had been raped, and I wasn't going to tell him anything else about it. He of course demanded answers, but I shut down. I was ok telling him what happened, but I knew better by this point to tell him anymore. I wanted to trust him, but knew I couldn't. I just didn't want to be alone. I didn't know what to do, or who to trust. I was so depressed and wanted to die, I even told him that. It didn't take long after we got back together that his behavior started up again. My family and friends expressed their concern for my safety and I knew it was time to make a plan to get out for good. I was also seeing a different therapist at this time who told me that his behavior resembles that of a narcissistic sociopath, and just like my therapist before him, he tells me to run.

I remember him getting mad at me because my dogs were in my bedroom, he hated my dogs and I wish I would have just broken up with him on that principle alone. He puts them on the deck of my apartment and we started fighting.

The fights started easier and intensified quickly. I remember looking at him and saying "you know if I end up dead, everyone will know it's you, right?" He smugly smiled and said "I know." He began breaking things, screaming and getting in my face. I told him he needed to leave my apartment, and he refused. This went on for a good 30 minutes or more. I said if he didn't leave I was going to call the cops. He began to make threats back about how he was going to ruin my career and my life if I picked up the phone. I believed him. I was living in fear all the time, and in this moment I was scared of what he was going to do to me. I went into my room and I got my baseball bat and told him one more time "get the fuck out of my house!' He left. I think he knew at that point, I was ready to snap. He wouldn't stop calling me.

He would leave voicemails screaming telling me to go kill myself and then leave 2 minute messages about how he didn't deserve this and I was abusive and how could I treat him like this.

I tried to smooth things over as best as I could to calm him down and try to make it up to him, but this was it for me. I was numb and it was time to get out of this mess. I came up with a plan had gotten everything lined up and I knew that the next time he blew up, all ties were cut. It was a matter of time and I started to distance myself from him again, which I knew would trigger him.

As expected, he called and demanded me to come over and see him, I said no. He began to tell me that if I didn't see him, he was going to sleep with someone else that night. I stopped reacting to his bullshit, I didn't care anymore and I was done, but what he said next was the nail in the coffin. The last thing he said to me was "only someone so pathetic would lie about getting raped for attention." I hung up the phone. I put my plan into action because I knew it was a matter of time before he showed up at my place. I already had a new changed my number, I changed cars with someone, and was able to break the lease at my apartment and move into a temporarily place only to move again 3 months later. I had a friend that knew what I had been going through and I felt safe and protected in their home.

I experienced a good amount of relief when I left, and I wish I could say I felt free at this time, but I didn't. I felt haunted by him, and by the memories of him. I felt like I was living in a constant state of fear. Fear of going back, fear of him finding me, as well as major depression from all of the other trauma. I began to drink heavily to numb the pain. It was so hard to find people that had gone through what I had gone through and when I did share my story with people, they were so uncomfortable. I felt so alone. It had been a year since I had left him and it was my birthday, and I was sad, drunk and alone, which seemed to be my comfort zone now. I received an email from a new an account that I didn't recognize. It was him, and was reaching out to me to tell me how sorry he was and said how much he missed me and that life wasn't the same without me. He proceeded to tell me how much he has been working on himself and he really is a changed man and would do anything to prove it to me. He wanted to apologize for everything he put me through.

That got to me, because he never apologized for anything, and I wanted an apology more than anything. I responded and didn't hold back. I told him I didn't believe him, and he had no idea how much he hurt me or what he had put me through. I immediately felt guilty for responding, I knew better. I know that there should be no contact, so I don't reply again.

Six months later I see him at a concert and leave immediately. He emails again and I ignore it. A couples months after a breakup from another man, he emails again. It was like he could smell my vulnerability in the air, like a shark smells blood in the water. This was a rough breakup for me and my drinking became worse. He asked to meet and at this point, I was so angry and full of resentment, I didn't really give a shit what happened to me. I wanted that Goddamn apology even more. I put so much work into leaving this man and years later I still want some type of closure. I wanted him to know that I didn't fear him anymore. Hindsight, it was such a stupid thing to do, but I'm glad I did it. I told a friend when/where I was meeting him. I drove a different car, and I went to a different location after.

There he was. I saw him and I instantly knew he was full of shit. I was repulsed by this man, he seemed to pathetic to me. I hadn't fully healed from this process, but I had grown a lot more than I gave myself credit for. He apologized, which meant nothing to me.

He told me he was moving out of state, which I looked up that he did end up selling his house. He gave me a bunch of music as a gift and I didn't feel like I owed him a thing, because I didn't. All the power he had over me was gone. I was almost free. I left and

never looked back. He sent me another
e-mail and I blocked his ass. It was time
to move on with my life. It took me
another 4 or 5 months of life still
throwing challenges my way, and I had
finally hit a breaking point in where I
knew I had to make some major
changes and really start healing.

I stopped drinking and started
therapy and going to AA. Working the
twelve steps has been changing my life.
I used drinking to repress all the pain of
years of abuse rather than facing it. I
was ready to get rid of my feelings of
worthlessness, insecurities and my fears
associated with men and intimacy. I
have been dealing with these issues on
the deepest level and I can finally say
now that I am freer than I ever have
been. I never knew life could be so
beautiful. I know my worth, and I stick
to my boundaries. I will never walk that

dark path again, because I found a light. I'm proud of who I've become in the process and I can say that I love myself now. I made it.

Survivor: C. Marie

*　*　*

I met him in June 2009. I was coming home from work that evening. I sat quietly alone on the train reading a book. A tall, dark, athletic, guy with pearly white teeth and a million dollar smile approached me and introduced himself. He had me at Hello!

He was someone I thought was Heaven sent. I thought he was also the man I always dreamed of having. His smile had me mesmerized; he touches, hugs and kisses felt so good. He used to sing to me. He had a very nice singing voice. He even wrote me poems and songs. He brought me gifts and made me feel like I was the only woman in the world. I was in love and nobody can me anything.

Three months later- The man I thought was my Knight in shining Armor turned out to be a nightmare. He was really a monster dressed in aluminum foil. The man that was once so loving, so kind, romantic and passionate was now evil, selfish, cruel, controlling and abusive in so many ways. He started showing his true colors and who he really was the first day he came to my place.

I invited him over one night after a few weeks of dating. He took it upon himself to extend the invitation. He was showing up unannounced. He was coming over every day and staying until the next morning. He would leave when I would go to work and come back that evening. I didn't mind at first but I did have a life outside of him like work, school, family and church on Sundays.

The encounter I had with him was the day I decided to tell him I need the weekend to focus. I been going to work late, missed two days of class when the semester just started. I was also behind in class assignments I needed to catch up with. Which was my main reason for wanting to focus. I had to keep canceling my sister and my lunch and spa dates we have one Saturday a month and Id been missing Church. All since we started dating.

"Oh! I see you're too busy for me. You have no time for me. Other things are more important. You don't love me like you say you do. I'm sorry I bothered you. But you don't ever have to worry about me anymore". He left my house after that. I called him but he sent me to voicemail. I told him," I was sorry if I made him feel bad. I should have just let him walk out and stay out forever. He called me two days later apologizing and saying he, "missed me and want to see me". Why did I agree?

I was back with him and things were OK not great. He was still coming over every day. I stopped going to class and to church. Shortly after the first encounter a second one followed weeks later.

The second one happened when I told him about an event my church has every year in the fall. I get excited as the time gets close and even bought my ticket months earlier. I told him about it weeks before. Three days before the event he asked, "Can I please not go"? I told him I already paid for a ticket and I been looking forward to this all year. "FINE!" He screamed so loud I thought my ears would pop." Then go"! He said standing up throwing a glass of ice water at the wall causing it to shatter in Millions of pieces. Let's say I didn't go. I had missed out on plenty more events after. Family gatherings, my nephew football games, and birthday parties. I needed permission and approval first.

If I did go anywhere he would call me every 15 minutes and rush me home. After two hours he say "I been out to long and I need to come home".

I never got to enjoy myself being anywhere. He wanted me up under him all day every day. I must answer my phone when he call or hell would break loose. If I missed his call because I was in the shower, at work, in with the doctor he accuse me of cheating. It was at a point where I had to bring my phone in the shower with me, keep it on when I'm at work (risking my job) , answering it if I'm in the dentist with them all in my mouth. I missed his call one day because I was in the middle of a dental procedure. I see 10 missed calls from him and 10 angry text messages. I told him I was at the dentist. He said I was lying and I was with some other man and hung up on me. I kept calling him telling him he has to believe me. He then said I was probably screwing the dentist. After 45 minutes of arguing and me stating my innocence case he said to bring him a note with the date and time on it saying I was there and he will believe me. I did it only for the simple fact that I had nothing to hide. I told him when I got home that, "I wanted to break up because I was tired of these arguments and accusations". Of course he apologized and promised he change. Of course I gave in. Things will be good for a few days then the abuse would always get worse.

When things didn't go his way he would get mad and call me all types of B's, whores and street walkers. He would tell me I don't do anything when I did everything. Cook, clean, wash his clothes, and give him money when he needed it. He would also tell me how I'm wasting my time with school because I'm stupid. I'm no good, I'm ugly, fat, slow, retarded and don't no man want me. He needs to find another woman. I'm not good enough for him. I told "if I'm not then leave my house. He started apologizing saying he didn't mean it the way he said it. How else could he have meant it?

He brainwashed me into believing I was ugly, worthless, stupid, a failure and nobody loved me. I don't do anything right. That is why all of my relationships failed. He told me my family don't love me or care about me that is why nobody comes to visit me. In reality he was the reason. Nobody like him because of his attitude. He said aside from him if they really loved me they still around come around for me. I started feeling depressed miserable stressed. Everything I touch got ruined

He was not only mentally abusing me but physically abusing me as well. I

suffered with frequent trips to ER. I
got kicked, punched, spit on, hit with
belts, wet towels, and hard objects. He
throw a cable remote at the back of my
head for not listening to him. He
always wanted to have sex and I was
forced to even when I didn't want to.

He would watch porn and tell me to
do what those women do. I couldn't. I
was no gymnasts. I couldn't do
handstands, splits, and flips and stuff.
He would try to put me in the positions
they were in. It would be painful. If I
yelled in pain or because I couldn't
breathe, He would get mad and punch
me. I had to act like nothing was wrong
and try my best to do what he says even
if I felt my neck would snap, or I'll
break my spine and I must get it right
and thing goes wrong. I would suffer
through punches in the face, head,
stomach or anywhere until I do it the

way he likes it or he decided to give up and just verbally attack me saying," You fat this, that. You need to go on a diet. You suck, you can't do nothing right. I need to find a woman to please me right. I gave him warnings about hitting me, saying if he keeps doing it, I'm leaving him. He begged me not to and promised me he won't hit me again. He did keep his promise for a week but each time he did things only got much more and worse.

I believed he was still a good person aside from everything. I knew he has a good side to him. I've seen it once before and was certain he would one day be the man I fell in love with again. We had some good days. Days when we would laugh and enjoy each other without fighting. On our good days I would try to talk to him and help me through things. Like better his life, find a job, and reach his goals. He had no ambition to find a job, he was in a comfort zone and thought life was perfect the way he was living now. He said he wasn't ready to go get his driver's license or GED. All he did was sit in my house or his brother house all day eating, playing video games and smoking. I even tried getting us both counseling in home. He agreed to it and we have one session together once a week then we have one on one the following week.

After our first session together. He said he wasn't attending anymore because it was a waste of people. He sat in my bedroom during my session one day and five minutes into the session he called me into the room telling me to kick the therapist out now. If I don't he will. I refuse to and begged him to not cause a scene. He said do it or you know. I did. After the woman gather her belongs and left, He stormed out the room tossing a wireless videogame controller at my head and throwing me on the ground kicking and stomping me asking," why I have people in our business". If I ever tell anyone again, call the police or anything he would kill me.

One month later he was on the phone talking to female. I went ballistic. I told him to leave. Now what if the shoe was the other foot? This is the same man that hit me hard in back a few weeks ago causing an injury because he found out I had a male doctor when I went to the doctors for a same day appointment because I was sick. He said why I allowed another man to touch me. He see my brothers or uncles saying they are some dudes

I'm screwing, the cable guy he claim I was flirting with because I told him to have a nice day. I gather the little bit of his belongings and started tossing them into a trash bag. He snatched the bag from me and punched me so hard it caused me to fall and spin around. My ear hurt really badly. I begin to vomit. The neighbor from downstairs knocked on our door asking if everything was OK. We told him everything was fine. I took a taxi to the hospital and turned out he somehow put a tear in my ear drum. Thank God the doctors were able to repair it. He cried when we got home saying how sorry he was and won't do it again. Yeah sure he always says that. Only this time I was at my wits end.

He is just going to keep doing what he doing again and again until he kills me. I will have more and more visits to the ER until the police were called. I was not excited about seeing him, or happy with him, I felt happier on workdays and looked forward to work days away from him. I would even tell him had to work on my days off just to get away from him for some hours. I was going to lose my job. I already suffered through many losses, my family, my friends, money, and school, Church, my house not being my home anymore, my pride, self-esteem, happiness, independence. I could have it all back and restore it all by just getting rid of what's and who's causing it. Him!

That evening after leaving the ER, I stayed up all night and had a long talk with him. I told him exactly how I felt. This is a dead end relationship or is it even a relationship? It seems more like a routine. We do the same thing, we eat the same thing. There is nothing exciting. We have absolutely nothing in common. We have no goals. You're not trying to do anything to better yourself. Like going back to school, get a job, driver license, and counseling. I can't keep taking the stress, beatings, emotional abuse. I need to get myself back together before it's too late. I told him I dealt with him and his mess for a year and I refused to take on another. He said his famous, I will do better line and this time he was serious.

He told me to call the woman back up and set up counseling for us again and he will get his GED and license and find a job because he can't afford to lose me. He had nobody else. No friends and his brother was talking about kicking him out and he won't have a place to stay if he does. I had no sympathy. I just said if you value me and love me you're take everything I said serious....... he didn't!

He was sweet that whole night selling me dreams about things we were going to do once he get a job. But that next morning he went crazy. He tuned into another person. A person I've never seen before.

I was in the bathroom getting ready for work. He walks in and shuts the door locking it looking at me with evil eyes. It was kind of scary. "Where you going?" he asked in an evil smirk like he had something up his sleeve. I thought he had a gun or knife and would kill me right then and there. 'To work.' I said terrified. He walked up on me saying "no you are not going nowhere you're going to give me some sex." He then started trying to pull down my pants. I starting yelling for him to stop saying I have to get to work. He said, F*** your job and knocked me to the ground. I started pushing him trying to make my way to the door. He grabbed me, punching me in my jaw, and kicking me in the stomach. I was in pain but I wasn't going to let him rape me. I was screaming for him to let me go, throwing punches, scratching and biting and kicking him. He then pinned me down to the ground so I couldn't get up and I just screamed and yelled not knowing I was yelling for help.

Then I heard a loud bang on my front door, cause him to stop. It was the police. The guy downstairs called because he heard all the screaming and reported a domestic disturbance. The police seen the bruises and marks all over my face and my swollen jaw. He was arrested and charged with aggravated assault and attempt to rape.

I moved 2 months later to a new house. I got a new phone. He was in jail and was not allowed to contact me on any circumstances. I thought he was out my life for good. Not quite!

He was out of jail and he called me one night. I don't know how he got my number. But he called me saying please don't hang up and just hear him out. He's sorry, he learned his lesson, he changed and he has to have me back. I yelled for him to stop calling me and hung up. He text me saying if he can't have me nobody ever will. The same way he got my new number he can get my address and come after me. I called the police. The police called the number he called me from but got no answer after a few attempts. He must have knew the police were after him ended up changing the number. We went back in court. He denied it being him calling me and sending those text messages. The judge said there was no proof it was him and threw out our case. So this man got away with assault, attempting to rape, violating a protective order and stalking.

My landlord agreed to install some cameras around my house in case he did show up. I changed my number again and I moved again but this time somewhere far. I have not received a phone call, text message or seen any sign of him since the day we left court.

It's been 6 years now. I went back to school in 2011 and received my bachelor degree in 2013. I am close with my family again and so glad to be back with them. I am back in church and I attend every Sunday faithfully. I am now helping women in domestic violence situations. I hate to see and hear anyone suffering the way I have for a year. I have not been dating or been back in another relationship since that last one. Maybe someday I will be, but when I do, I promise myself not to end up with another man like him. I hope we never meet again!

👑 Survivor: Tia

*　　*　　*

I met my ex abuser in the prime of my life. I was 21 and had just bought myself my first house and a new car. I was in a great job, and was studying to further my career.

He was a bad boy who I wanted to turn good. I honestly wanted to help him change his life. I let him sleep on

my couch, put a roof over his head and
made sure he was reasonably well fed.
He'd help me around the house and
found himself a decent job. He was
changing his life for the better, and I
was really proud of him. We ended up
falling in love and not long after, I fell
pregnant. It was after That's when the
abuse started, I have no idea why it
started, perhaps it was because he felt
that since we had the tie of a baby
between us that I was his possession,
and should do as he pleased. The abuse
started off with name calling and
insults, but soon progressed to isolating
me from my family and friends and
accusing me of sleeping with other
people to justify himself in calling me
harsh names. Every day he would say
that the baby wasn't his and that I'd
slept with my co-workers.

Slowly but surely the all the insults and trying to appease him stripped away the confident, self assured young woman I once was. I was left an empty shell whose days were spent trying to please him in any way. I could and almost always walking on eggshells. Nothing I did was ever right or good enough and I ended up believing I was useless and good for nothing.

The abuse then quickly became violent. It started with a kick in my back when I was pregnant, then escalated to punching, choking and dragging me around by the hair. His level of control included raping me several times daily. I remember once when I was about 5 months pregnant we were going on a picnic. I packed a lunch and started driving to find a nice park to have it. I was led to drive into the middle of nowhere, far away out into the deserted bush where I was forced to lean over a large rock and was raped repeatedly. I was begging him to stop because it was hurting me and the baby. He was relentless. It was at that very moment where it dawned on me that he could end up killing me.

The rest of the pregnancy was a blur. I was trying to hold down a job while getting sick, He lost his job and I ended up paying all the bills. He had taken my bank card and managed all the finances. He put buying pot and cigarettes a priority over paying bills and putting food on the table. I had to rely on sneaky tactics and my parents to keep the electricity, house and car payments.

Once my daughter was born I thought things might change for the better. Life was great for the first week home. We were a happy family, but it all soon turned to shit and the violence and abuse came back tenfold. I was forced to go back to work full time; two weeks after giving birth. While I was lucky enough that I could go home at lunch to be with her, I also had to endure violent non-consensual sex. The heartache I felt every day leaving my beautiful new born in his care was unbearable but there was nothing I could do. A couple of times I came home and he had bitten or hurt her and he always explained that it was an accident. I had absolutely no strength and no control over my life and yet I couldn't find the strength to protect my own innocent flesh and blood who relied on me for her life. These were the darkest of times.

The days and weeks became really blurry and every day was filled with violence of some kind. I remember moments that stand out and even now, whilst writing, other vicious moments come out from my subconscious. Rocking me to my core. Moments like kneeling on the floor with my baby in my arms whilst he stands behind me pulling my hair back with one hand and a knife at my neck, with the other. I was strangled until I was unconscious. I remember feeling the peacefulness and serenity of the small escape from my reality. I would be motionless on the floor with him leaning over me yelling that I'm a liar and faking it.

My daughter's first Christmas was spent with me being raped and beaten from 3 am and the police landing on my doorstep at 7 am to say the neighbors have called them about all the fighting. All my neighbors were well aware of what was going on, they were witness to it. In broad daylight he would drag me by the hair out of the house and dump me on the road whilst only wearing my underwear, would jump up and down on my car whilst I tried to drive away.

The violence didn't just penetrate my own household, it also penetrated my mum and dad's. They knew what was going on but because felt hopeless to help me. On one occasion after being beaten and having my nose bitten I had barricaded myself in the bathroom so I could cleanse myself and clean my nose out. For some reason at that point my mum called and I begged her to come over. When she got there she found tosog out the back trying to hang himself in the shed and me in the house nursing my baby trying to clean myself up. The police had come as well. The neighbors had called them again.

They asked me in front of him if I wanted them to take him away for the night. My heart ached for them to take him away, but I knew if I said yes, that I would have to deal with the consequences when he returned. In the end I said no and that everything would be ok.

Mum and dad tried to talk to me about leaving but I only made excuses for him. There was nothing else they could do apart from try to talk sense into me which wasn't going to happen. In my warped mind there was no other option but to stay and live with the knowledge that my life would soon be taken from me but hopefully my daughter's would be spared and she would be able to be brought up by my parents whilst he rotted in jail for murder.

I stayed with him until my daughter was 8 months. I don't know what the catalyst was that gave me the strength to leave, I just remember finding out that there was a free counseling service up the road from where I was living. I eventually found a believable excuse to go up there. I told him that I was going to see if they could help financially with paying a bill so we could keep our power on. I knew he wouldn't go because it was 'below' him to seek charity.

Once I got into her office I broke down and told her everything. She worked with me in the short time that I had and we had a plan in place for when I was ready to leave. The power and pride I felt walking out of there knowing that I was taking my life and that of my daughters back was amazing. For the first time in ages I felt empowered and in control of my destiny. A week later after another horrible night of rape, abuse and being dragged naked out onto the road, I'd had enough.

I calmly got ready for work and as soon as I was there rang my mum, gave her the number of the counselor and told her to have the police ready for when I finished work.

On the bus home from work I was petrified and nervous but excited. I got off a few stops early and ran as fast as I could to the counselor's office. I knew by the time I got there he would know something was up. He'd wait for me at the bus stop everyday and there was no way I'd ever miss the bus because it wasn't worth the hell.

At the counselors office I met up with my mum, the police and the counselor. The police took my address and asked for a description. Out the front of the office I spotted him walking with the stroller up to the shops to come and look for me. The police went to him, took my daughter from him and told him he had 5 minutes to get back to the house and to clear his shit and get out. I had to go there with them and it was one of the liberating yet scary things I've ever done. After he left I gathered up some of my own stuff and left the house, there was no way I could stay there. I needed security and to be around people who would protect me. I moved into my parent's dining room for a while but would go home to make sure that everything was ok. I'm sure he'd been back and was doing things to scare me. Eventually I had to go home. At home I would barricade all the doors and windows, would have knives and constantly lived on edge – I was no longer living with the abuse but I was still living with the fear.

The day after he was removed from our lives I went straight to legal aid to seek a DVO. It was rushed through and I found myself in a closed courtroom with the lawyer and a judge. The judge asked me a couple of questions and then said that he didn't need to hear anything else and granted me the DVO on the spot. The DVO was served onto him on Valentine's day, when the court hearing date came around, the VRO went uncontested so was finalized and put into place for two years.

Since the day the police removed him, I've never seen him again. For the first year he would send my daughter a birthday card with messages that were directed at me but he has never tried to seek contact with my daughter.

Today I still live with the fear although now it doesn't consume me. I went through a DV women's group run by Relationships Australia which helped me to understand the violence and taught me that it wasn't my fault, I learnt to recognize the cycle of violence and to change the negative thoughts that were going through my head with positive thoughts so I could rebuild my self esteem and value.

My daughter and I now live in a family where she knows that the man she calls dad isn't her biological dad and that her real dad hurt me and made me cry. She knows that when she's older if she wants to find him I will do everything in my power to find him. As she gets older I have told her more and more of my history, I know she will have to make her own mistakes but I hope I can spare her from going through what we did and she will learn this lesson from my mistakes.

👑 Survivor: Sharon Rea

July of 89 – Boy did I ever feel like the adult I always wanted to be. Out on my own, go anywhere I want to without a curfew! I was ecstatic! I met the man I thought would be "the one" during this month, April. We met one evening when a friend and I were out cruising. He yelled at us to pull over, so we did.

WOW! He was charming, understanding and so intelligent.

Over the next two months we saw each other whenever we could. He seemed so perfect in my eyes. Everything was great! We moved in together in November, and things were going so well.

One evening we went to see his brother at the basketball courts. His brother hadn't arrived yet, so we sat in the car talking. I can't remember what we were talking about, but I remember him pushing the side of my head so hard it hit the side of the window. I started crying. No one had ever touched me that way and it shocked me. I cried and cried and he said, "I barely touched you, get over it." That should have been the first red flag.

How did I justify it? I told myself, "Well, he was just kidding, he didn't mean to hit me that hard."

A few days later I found out he was cheating on me! I was furious and hurt and questioned myself as to what I did. I kept my voice silent for awhile. I didn't let him know I knew and I began making plans to leave his butt high and dry. On the second day of his new job, my friends and family rented a U-Haul and I packed all the furniture. I had only left him a fork, spoon, knife, plate, blanket and pillow.

I was gone a month when he figured out where I was and started phoning me constantly until I finally just decided to go back. He had sweet talked me yet again. I had friends from my hometown write me in Pennsylvania to give me encouragement.

When I came home, he was sweet as candy (the honeymoon phase). A week later we were married on December 12th. The following week a letter came for me that was forwarded from my PA address. He said he had opened it because he could tell it was a man's handwriting.

He came to my workplace, a nursing home, and we stepped outside. He immediately punched me as hard as he could right in the middle of my chest! I could only gasp for breath! He was showing me parts of the letter and would force me to read it out loud and smash the letter in my face. The head nurse came outside to see if I was okay.

She saw me doubled over and brought me a bag to breathe in and suggested that he leave. After he left, my co-workers begged me not to go home with him, but I was afraid not to. I was afraid that he would find me and kill me.

When he came to pick me up, I had barely gotten in the car before he was grabbing my hair and yanking my head every which way he could. As he drove, he would slap my face with his open hand over and over. He punched me in the chest multiple times. It went on until we got home, which was a 30 minutes away. He was in the apartment before I was and yelled back to me that my "ass better get in here, don't make me come back to get you." Until he said that, I was planning on going to the neighbors behind us, but didn't want him causing any trouble for them.

The next few hours he threw the home phone and made a perfect imprint on the top of my left leg. He'd walk by me to go in the kitchen or bathroom and bust my in the face on the way, or he'd grab my hair and yank it so hard I would end up in the floor in a heap! When bed time came, I was on the couch and he was already in the "sweet" mood and he wanted us to sleep under the Christmas tree. I kept my eyes closed and didn't move the whole night.

The next morning all I heard was him saying, "Oh God, what have I done", "I'm so sorry." I went to the bathroom and there wasn't a place on me that wasn't black or blue. I looked like the "elephant man." I could hardly

look at myself! He told me I wasn't
going to work that night and I told him
if he wanted money at pay day that he'd
better let me go.

When I walked into my workplace
they all gasped and shook their heads
and had me work in areas where no
people could see me. During that time,
my co-workers took pictures of me and
I called the cops and told them when
he was to come and pick me up. They
took more pictures, took my statement
and waited for his arrival. The blocked
him in and arrested him and also
confiscated a gun.

Over the next few years I left him 6 or
7 times. He was put in jail at least 3
times. During these years he had
chipped my tooth, hit me so hard I slid
over the coffee table and landed in the

floor, threw his keys at me and hit me right between the eyes leaving me a bloody mess and a nice scar. He also had hit me so hard open handed on the forehead that it knocked me out. When I came too, he was dragging me through the living room into the kitchen area and trying to throw water on me so wake up. As I came too all I saw was all my blood mixing with the water and down the drain.

At the last part of our marriage, I finally quit getting mad when he wanted to "go out" and also when he came in at 5 in the morning. Then he'd get mad at me because he'd think I was the one up to something! Towards the end of the marriage I got to the point of fantasizing about digging his grave and putting him in it, laughing as I shoveled dirt back into the hole and spitting on his grave and laughing all the way back to my car. But I realized that would be putting myself on his level and I'd never treat others like I've been treated.

As fate would have it, the next day as he was going "out," he said a statement that really hurt me more than the hitting ever did. He said, "Why don't you just go ahead and kill yourself and make my life easier." My mouth dropped open and I stood in shock! After all he put me through, this one statement is the only thing that really validated in my mind that I did deserve better. That my life wasn't meant to be abused, to be isolated and just feeling like nothing.

I imagined I was a caged bird being let out to freedom and I know I was going to fly as fast and as high as I could go, flapping my wings, doing flips and chirping my little heart away in a song of joy that I'd be singing for the rest of my life. Experiencing all that I have, I am quite proud of who I am today. Each time I talk to individuals I always start with "I am a survivor." I'm not going to say I haven't struggled, but when I remind myself of not having to walk on eggshells and that I'm free to be my own person who can make decisions on her own, I feel like shouting it out to the whole world.

I'm actually finding the girl I was before I got married, except this one is stronger, not afraid to ask for help and I let my voice be heard! God has never let me go, he's been with me through thick and thin and I count my blessings every day! If I can come through this, I have no doubt that others can too.

Look at it like this, you have a clean slate now and a new beginning at life…be whatever you want to be, go back to school, stand tall and proud, and most of all LOVE YOURSELF!! It's your time to shine like the diamond you were meant to be, remember; don't give up. Reach out to others.

Know your worth and welcome it. Trust your gut and always remember the way people give up their power is by thinking you don't have any.

👑 **Survivor: Jennifer A.**

*　　*　　*

I met my ex-abuser in 5th grade. I had known this guy from the age of 13 to the age of 17-20. We were at first very much in love and inseparable. My ex abuser had ADHD, bipolar, depression, and manic depression.

From 2013-2014 we dated off and on. His mom was always involved and in the way, she was a big part of why we always argued and how she would rage the fire and anger inside of him. She would make up false things against me and try to solve the problems, when it wasn't her position to do so. He would get his mom involved in a lot of our privacy and our relationship issues and i felt it was ridiculous. He told his mom things and things that were private and he wouldn't stop her. He did get mad at her in the past when we were dating.

We dated off and on but this last time was the final straw. 2015 in April we started talking and his mom was mad that we had started talking. Once his mom was mad then his attitude changed. He was happy to be in my life again and so was I. But never did I or would I of ever thought that he would mentally and physically abuse me.

Never did I think he would of taken off and he would of never spoke to me again and blamed the violence on me. Right? Always blaming the victim? May 2015 came the night the incident happened. He was acting off I wasn't sure what was wrong with him. He was very quiet and I didn't know how to help him. He started hitting me and trying to get me to have sex with him. This was NO sexual hitting.

He started slapping me and choking me and I could hardly breathe. He said I was going to take the hits he beaten me from the waist down, and my neck was swollen. He got up and started yelling at me saying that I was talking about his mom. My parents heard and came running upstairs. He wasn't making sense and he took off, my dad went to look for him but he was nowhere to be found. We called his parents they didn't know where he was and his mom wasn't concerned one bit. He had hidden my phone and took some violent pictures of me bruised.

Short story his parents had no concern about me and didn't care, they didn't make him take any responsibility and they knew he had been videotaping me and disgusting things. He was never charged and got away with it. He tells people only some of the story, not all of it. Don't the abusers always play the victim?

I had run into him not to long ago and he came up to my dad, and I confronted him. It felt good to gain the power back that he had taken from me.

Needless to say he's a low life and has no career going for him. None of it

makes sense to what happened. But I
am free of him.

Survivor: Michaela B.

"Someone I loved once gave me a box full of darkness. It took me years to understand that this too, was a gift."
– Mary Oliver

*   *   *

No one really tells you what life is like after you have escaped your abuser, fled your home, let your life as you once knew it behind. I thought the hardest part was behind me, after all, life with my abuser was filled with terror, threats, beatings, rapes, mind games, and a constant fear that I would never live to see the next day. What I did not realize is that life after abuse comes with its own set of challenges and difficulties. The abuse that I endured has completely changed everything about me. I have transformed into an entirely new person and been forced to mourn the loss of my former self. During this transformation period, I have been forced to deal with many new demons and issues. While this has been an extremely difficult road to travel, it has also been one of the most rewarding experiences of my life. I have found an unwavering appreciation for the little things in life and been able to successfully find my way to happiness again.

I had known my abuser for twenty years and we were childhood friends. We dated off and on over the years, but he had never exhibited any indication to me that he would be violent. At the time, I didn't know anything about Domestic Violence and I didn't know the warning signs, so I didn't realize that his extreme jealousy was a sign that something was really wrong. The final time we dated, we lived together for a year. In the beginning, it was the same as the other times we had dated...him accusing me of cheating on him, him being pissed that I had male friends, him going through my phone, him reading all my texts, him reading all my emails, him calling me a whore when a guy friend would text me, him being positive I cheated if I was home late, him refusing to let me see my friends unsupervised. I put up with it primarily because I wasn't cheating on him and truly deeply believed there was a way I could prove it to him and then our relationship would be fine. However, things never got better no matter what

I tried and three months into our relationship I told him I was done and he needed to take his things and get out of my apartment. His reaction was absolutely terrifying. He punched holes in the walls. He pinned me down on the bed so I couldn't move, told me we were never going to break up. He threatened to destroy everything I own if I left him. He kept me trapped in the room for hours until I agreed to take back what I said. After that day, everything changed. He knew I wanted out and he was determined to make sure I stayed. The last nine months of our relationship were pure hell. He became increasingly violent. He would hit me, kick me, throw me onto the floor, punch me, trap me in rooms, slam my head into absolutely anything, rape me, tell me that if I ever left him he would kill me. And I believed it. I had never felt so trapped and alone in my entire life. I thought I was going to die in that relationship. I thought there was no way out.

The day of the final assault changed everything for me. He had me pinned down on the kitchen floor and his hands were wrapped tight around my neck. I could not breathe. His eyes were completely vacant. I knew he was going to kill me, I could tell by his expressionless face, his dead eyes, how hard he was gripping my neck. This man, who swore he loved me, is about to murder me. On the counter, I can see my phone. I make a decision. Get to that phone and call someone. I called a friend. This immediately calms him down because now he is worried. I had been so busy the entire year trying to hide my abuse from everyone and now all the sudden I am telling someone else what is going on in our relationship. He is suddenly on his best behavior. My friend and I plot a plan of escape and I report my assault to the police. Four days after he strangled me, I flee our home and he is arrested for strangulation and assault in the fourth degree.

My healing journey has been an extremely difficult road. When I first fled him, I had the most intense fear all of the time. Fear that I would run into him somewhere in public, fear that I would freeze with terror if I saw him, and fear that he would follow through on his threat to kill me. I had fled to a new city and he had no idea where I was living. And yet, every night I would have the same nightmare over and over...he would break into my home while I was gone and be waiting for me in my bedroom. Once I walked in, he would shoot me. I would wake up in sheer terror. Going out in public became more and more difficult and being in crowds was just unbearable. I was still under extremely high stress and continued living in fight or flight mode for a very long time.

About six months into our relationship, he punched me in the face and knocked me unconscious. I suffered a concussion but it was never treated because I refused to let anyone know I was in an abusive relationship. During the course of our relationship, he has probably slammed my head into various objects hundreds of times. The result of all this has left me with frequent headaches and memory loss.

One of the hardest parts of life after abuse is my constant battle with self-esteem, depression and anxiety. I struggle every single day with my feelings of value and worth. I struggle because my own boyfriend punched me in the face and called me a Bitch as I lost consciousness, my own boyfriend told me he thought he had killed me during one assault and said it with no concern in his voice, my own boyfriend laughed in my face while he raped me and I screamed for him to stop, my own boyfriend tried to strangle me to death, my own boyfriend proved to me I am completely and utterly worthless. After all, if I was worth anything, he never would have done those things to me right? My battle with my worth forced me into a depression that I have struggled to escape from. Every single day I have to remind myself to love myself, to go easy on myself, to remember that he did this because he is a tortured terrible entity from hell and that it isn't my fault.

The most challenging part of being an abuse survivor for me, has been the total loss of self. I have lost everything that I used to be and have had to accept that the old me is completely and forever gone. My view of what I thought was 'real' was gone, my ability to trust was gone, my way of viewing the world was gone, the way I approached relationships and friendships was all gone. I had to rebuild everything in my life from scratch. I had to get to know the new me. I had to relearn how to trust. I had to relearn how to navigate through life. I had to relearn how to feel safe. I had to relearn to do pretty much everything without doubting my own decisions.

While this has been an extremely challenging journey for me, it has brought with it some of the greatest moments of my life. Most people do not get the opportunity to step back and look at their whole lives....how they were living, what they would change. This experience has forced me to examine everything about my life and the decisions that led me to this point. This experience has forced me to understand who I used to be, so that I can strive to make the new me a better person. Before abuse, I never noticed the little things, I never really cared.

Now, every single moment is precious to me. Every single sunrise that I get to see, every flower I get to smell, every time I get to sit next to a fire and feel warm, every second I spend with someone I love. all of it. Everything. It is huge to me. These are the moments that matter so very much now.

I have spent the bulk of my time learning about abuse and abusers, and attempting to get the warning signs out there so that people don't ever have to experience what I did. I don't ever want anyone to have to go through that. But I can say with complete honesty that I have made peace with my past and believe it has made me who I am today. Despite all of the difficulties during the healing journey, I am grateful for who I am today, I am grateful for the second chance that I have been given. Despite struggling with depression and self-esteem, I am truly happy.

I have found love. I have begun creating my new "normal." And what is great about this time of my life, is that I can create the new me and the new normal any way that I want. The healing journey is certainly filled with unexpected struggles but it is also so very rewarding if you are willing to look for all the good things in your life. My abuser took an entire year of my life and I will not allow him to have any more of it. I do not forgive him, but I have forgiven myself for not seeing the warning signs. There's nothing I can do now but to have the happiest most fulfilling life. This is my second chance and I want nothing more than to enjoy it and move on.

 **Survivor: Laura Polson**

I remember the first time I laid eyes on him like it was yesterday. He was standing on his parents steps 6'1 smooth dark skin, eyes that seemed like they were looking right through you and a smile that would melt your heart. At that very moment I knew this was a man I wanted to know. During this time I was seeing a man who had walked away from everything he had to be with me. At 18 I don't think you really know what you want out of life. I risked losing everything for one night with V.J. and that encounter changed my life forever. This was the beginning to a domino effect for everyone involved.

I kept telling myself this was a bad idea but I just couldn't get him out of my head. I go back to the night when everything changed. He was sitting at the table looking at me with those eyes and I was thinking this is my chance to see where this goes. Everything in my mind was telling me not to pursue this but I threw all of that out the window and went for him anyway. I ended up spending the night with him and walked away with more than I bargained for. I was drawn to him like a person drawn to a drug. We began sneaking around in the hopes that no one would find out about us. But like the saying goes what's done in the dark will always come to the light. There was excitement in all of this for me but I was not prepared for what was to come. I soon found out that I was pregnant now what am I going to do? Now I had to figure out how I was going to look this other man in the face and tell him I was carrying V.J. baby. Now came the hard part for me telling both of these men life changing news.

So, here I go with this news. One was going to be hurt by my actions and disregard for his feelings. The other one I wasn't sure how he would take the news. I was young and scared cause I really didn't know what the future held for me. Would he stand by me or would I do this alone? I finally told V.J. that he was going to be a father again and he seemed to be overjoyed. See at the time he was already raising his son alone. This gave me hope that he would be a great father because I watched him be that to his son. So we decided to come together as a family and make this work. Everything was all love in the beginning. He was there right by side going to my appointments with bells on. We would sit on the couch watching tv while he would rub my stomach and talk to the baby. I was in heaven thinking could it get any better than this. Then when I was about 7 months he left me to go work in another city. While he was away I didn't really hear from him which made me feel alone. I had a hard time during the end and thought I would lose my child but God stepped in. I gave birth to a beautiful little girl all without her father being there.

V.J. came back about 2 weeks after I gave birth. I was so angry with him because he left me to do this all alone.

But the moment that I saw him all of that went out of the window and I let him right back in without a second thought. He was like a drug to me and I couldn't walk away. See I knew what it was like to come from a broken home and I didn't want the same fate for my daughter. I wanted her to know what it was to have two parents that loved each other and her. So I did whatever I had to in order for it to work. Soon after I found myself pregnant again. I was 18 with two kids and another on the way. This was not the life that I saw for myself so I made a decision that would change me for a long time to come. I went on to have an abortion against everything he wanted me to do.

I believe that was when things began to change for us. He said he was okay but deep down I know he was angry with me. For a while he was kind

of distant to me. He was awesome with
the kids spending all of his time with
them but he looked at me a little
different. I found myself hanging with
my girlfriends more because I felt like
they could understand me just a little
better than he could. He hated the time
I spent with them because he felt like I
should be home with the kids. This is
where I began to see things change
between us . The fighting starts now
but I never really saw it as abuse.

I can recall one night I went out
with my friends which I had to lie in
order to go. Somehow he found out
that I went to the club and showed up
there. My friend was standing in front
of me and I saw the look on her face.
Right then I knew he was standing
behind me and this fear came across
me. When I turned around and looked
at him I knew it would be a long night.

We began to argue and all of sudden he grabbed me by my throat and pushed me out of the door. I feel to the ground and was waiting for someone anyone to help me but they didn't. He dragged me to the car and we left. That night I saw a man I was not use to seeing. But this would just be the start of many more to come.

We had good times, bad times and the times in between. The fights became harsh they were verbal and physical at times. Some moments are hard to relive. The sad thing is that during this time I'm not even sure that I knew something was wrong in our relationship. This was some what normal to me. For me if he wasn't upset about where I had been or what I was doing he didn't care. You can grow up seeing dysfunction and think it is the way things should be. See he hadn't hit me yet so I didn't think it was abuse. But I later learned that I was still being abused.

There was a time I wanted to go shopping with my girl friends and he said that I couldn't go. Of course I was thinking I am a grown woman and I will go wherever I want to. My grandmother was babysitting so what do I need his permission for? Let me just tell you that we got into a heated argument that let to him kicking the window out of my car. He then jumped in through the window and tried to throw the car into park. I jammed on breaks causing his legs to get cut on the glass. When he climbed out I took off, I bumped him with my car and he feel in the ditch. I drove home as fast as I could without looking back.

Another time we had an issue which always seemed to flow around me wanting to go out. He was so mad with me and I was feed up with his mess. I remember us screaming at one another, he was driving but he was so enraged.

Driving down this dead end road I knew this night would end badly. Once we parked he got out of the car then came around to my side and pulled me out. The words that came from the both of us were so toxic they could have killed. I was thinking to myself if you just be quiet maybe he would calm down but of course I keep going. Before I knew it his hands were around my neck. He choking me and I was still fighting him with all that I had. He let go then I felt this sting and burn come across my arm then my legs.

He was hitting me with a branch. I couldn't do anything but cry and beg him to stop. Which he did then he pinned me down to the hood of the car, pulled my pants down and raped me.

In my mind I couldn't believe this was happening and I thought because we were a couple it couldn't be rape. I later went to my cousins' house where I shared with her what happened. She ran me a hot tub of water and I sat there in tears as she took care of me that night.

I couldn't go to work for days because I was in so much pain. When I did go to work I had to cover all of the bruises so no one at work would see them. My supervisor called me out and said you know I that you have bruises again. I tried to play dumb to what she was talking about. She said, " Christina this can not keep going on. Do you realize that you are being abused?" For the first time things were real for me.

One day I made the decision that it would be best to end the relationship and that was what I did. And we seemed to be working things out for a few weeks. Then one night he called me and told me to come pick up our daughter because he wanted to go out. My cousin told me she would go but I said no because I knew how he felt about her. Well I drove to his house and he was outside waiting for me. The moment he turned around I knew I was in trouble. I was like God please don't let me die tonight. He jumped in the car and put a knife to my throat. At that moment I didn't know what was going to happen. He told me to drive and I did just what he said. I drove down this dead end road and parked like he told me to. We were there for hours that night and I was thinking I was never going to get out alive.

That night I was raped and stabbed 3 times in the chest. He was willing to let me die that night but I was determined that I was not going to leave my daughter without a mother. I began to think of ways to get away from him. So I told him that I loved him and that I knew he was sorry. I ensured him that I knew he didn't mean to hurt me. That's when I told him we could come up with a plan to make it look like I picked up someone and he was the one that assaulted me. And yes he went along with the plan. We drove back to his house where he went in and washed the knife off with bleach. Which to this day I can't stand the smell of. I crawled over to the driver side and drove down the street to my cousin's house. I then climbed out and knocked on the door. When the door opened I clasped knowing I had made it to safety. I was later taken to the hospital where the police came and took my statement.

I am now in a great place in life. Helping other women is my passion. I am now a Christian Coach, speaker and mentor. I live to show women that there is life after abuse. But most importantly I share my story of forgiveness. I was able to come to a place where I could forgive V.J. for all that he put me through. I love the woman who looks back at me in the mirror everyday because there was a time that I didn't like here. I am no longer battling with depression or drugs. I have truly been set free!!! V.J. and I share a great friendship where we

are grandparents to a handsome little
boy. He supports me sharing our story
with other women because he realized
that this was how I made it through. He
has become a humble man that has
faced his demons some of which we
faced together. I am thankful to be
walking in forgiveness because it freed
me to truly heal. In healing I am able to
help others walk into that same place.
Do not be held in bondage to what
happened by not being able to forgive.
Once you forgive you take your power
back. Remember forgiving is not about
the other person but it is about walking
in freedom for yourself.

🤴 **Survivor: Christina**

My story began like a fairy tale. Like most romances do. We met as teenagers and went to High school for a year together. I always had a secret crush on him but I was so over confident at 13 that I only dated older boys.

Throughout the years our paths crossed. Than when I was in my 20's I heard he was arrested and charged with Rape. I never really gave it any thought. Or thought much about him. I remember not being shocked when he was sentenced to Prison. He was always know as "the good looking guy" but was also labeled as being very angry and aggressive.

Flash forward to 34. I was walking down second avenue and I saw someone who looked very familiar. I stopped in my tracks and took a second glance and realized that it was Eric. At first I thought he looked horrible as if time had really done him injustice. I kept waking up to my apt. About 20 minutes later I came out and there he was on my corner. My heart started pounding. Yet neither one of us said a word to each other. I felt like a teenager again. All I kept thinking about was him for the next few days.

Ironically he had added me on FB prior to me seeing him. So I messaged him that I saw him. He later said oh wow! Small word. We made plans to see each other but each time I broke them. Finally, I agreed to meet him. It was as if time had stopped. We went to dinner and spent the night together. Deep down inside I felt like I was living out a teenage fantasy.

We talked for weeks and saw each other. Nothing really manifested until about a year later. Eric moved in with me. And at that time I felt like I was living on a cloud. Everything felt good. Sadly or not sadly a lot of people stopped talking to me as soon as they found out about my relationship.

Looking back I was in such euphoria that I didn't care. Here I was living with a Sexual Offender. Clearly something was wrong with me that I somehow managed to convince myself like he did with all his girlfriends that he was wrongfully convicted.

So what started out as a fairly tail ended up being a nightmare. I don't recall how long it took for him to lose control I just remember the look in his eye. He and I had a very tumultuous relationship. We were both easily set off. I won't forget the first time he hit me. He had been drinking and came home and out of nowhere started with me.

I ended up locking myself in my bedroom. He kicked in the door and started yelling at me. Then he hit me and wouldn't stop.

I didn't fight back. I just took it. He stopped and left the bedroom and then started hysterically crying. Somehow I blamed myself. From that day on it just got worse. I became angry and either would instigate a fight or I would fight back when he hit me.

Eric also had sexual issues. He would watch porn and masturbate up to 10 times a day. He did not care if I saw him. That only made me feel worse about myself.

I don't know what was my lowest point. Maybe him hitting with a belt, giving me two black eyes, stealing all of my designer handbags. I can't recall. Somehow I knew i had to end things. I eventually broke up with him. Kicked him out and moved.

We have been broken up for almost three years and I tried to move on. When you have been in a codependent relationship it feels normal. I gave in about a year ago and saw him. Nothing physicality or sexual occurred. It felt good almost like a drug.

Later on I learned that he used my new address for his resignation. Time went by and we talked. Nothing serious just friend talk.

This January he came to stay with me for a few days. I didn't even think about the past. On January 28 I came home and he was on my couch and he had the same look in his eye that he would get when he was ready to hit me.

I took my coat off. Next thing I remember he pushes me up against the wall in my kitchen. Eventually I feel to the floor and hit my head. He then takes out a knife and another weapon. Covers my mouth so I can't breathe and says do you like your teeth? Then he starts punching me in the stomach. Than says don't fight me. You have no idea what I am capable of. Continues to cover my mouth several times. Than drags me into the living room. Where he continued to punch me in the stomach. Suddenly out of nowhere he stopped. He sat on the couch and broke down and said he needed me.

I just looked at him. I gave him a Valium so that he could calm down. When I was assured that he was asleep I got out of the apartment and called the police. I had never done that before. I was exhausted and just wanted out. The police came and arrested him. We are now in court. I can't explain or try to make sense of this to a normal person. All I know is that when you are in a relationship even when it's over there is nothing more intoxicating. Now I know that i dated him because I never felt good about myself. I'm in therapy and trying to move on and be the happy person I know I can be.

No woman deserves to be hit, emotional verbalized. All I can say is that this is not love.
It's toxic and sad. It takes courage to leave. I respect anyone who tries. Might take a few times. My hope is that you get out before it's too late. So many women sadly don't get out in time. They either stay or they die. Don't let your emotions run your life. I did for so long. There is no shame in getting help.

Every day is a struggle. It gets easier and there is hope. You just have to believe in yourself.

♛ **Survivor: Tracy M.**

"Has he ever trapped you in a room and not let you out? Has he ever raised a fist as if he were going to hit you? Has he ever thrown an object that hit you or nearly did? Has he ever held you down or grabbed you to restrain you? Has he ever shoved, poked, or grabbed you? Has he ever threatened to hurt you?

If the answer to any of these questions is yes, then we can stop wondering whether he'll ever be violent; he already has been."
— Lundy Bancroft, Why Does He Do That?: Inside the Minds of Angry and Controlling Men

"Now let's move on to the subject of how a real man treats his wife. A real man doesn't slap even a ten-dollar hooker around, if he's got any self respect, much less hurt his own woman. Much less ten times over the mother of his kids. A real man busts his ass to feed his family, fights for them if he has to, dies for them if he has to. And he treats his wife with respect every day of his life, treats her like a queen - the queen of the home she makes for their children."

— S.M. Stirling, Dies the Fire

"The abusive man's high entitlement leads him to have unfair and unreasonable expectations, so that the relationship revolves around his demands. His attitude is: "You owe me." For each ounce he gives, he wants a pound in return. He wants his partner to devote herself fully to catering to him, even if it means that her own needs — or her children's — get neglected. You can pour all your energy into keeping your partner content, but if he has this mind-set, he'll never be satisfied for long. And he will keep feeling that you are controlling him, because he doesn't believe that you should set any limits on his conduct or insist that he meet his responsibilities."

— **Lundy Bancroft, Why Does He Do That?: Inside the Minds of Angry and Controlling Men**

"I am living in hell from one day to the next. But there is nothing I can do to escape. I don't know where I would go if I did. I feel utterly powerless, and that feeling is my prison. I entered of my own free will, I locked the door, and I threw away the key."

— **Haruki Murakami**

"The guarantee of safety in a battering relationship can never be based upon a promise from the perpetrator, no matter how heartfelt. Rather, it must be based upon the self-protective capability of the victim. Until the victim has developed a detailed and realistic contingency plan and has demonstrated her ability to carry it out, she remains in danger of repeated abuse."
— **Judith Lewis Herman**, **Trauma and Recovery**

"My father was one of those men who sit in a room and you can feel it: the simmer, the sense of some unpredictable force that might, at any moment, break loose, and do something terrible.
[Burnside, p. 27]"

— John Burnside, A Lie About My Father: A Memoir

"What are you going to do? Are you going to live in the dark, locked in here? Afraid to look out, answer the door, leave? Yes, he's out there, and he's clearly not going to leave you alone until one of three things happens: he hurts you and gets arrested, or he makes a mistake and gets arrested, or you stop him."

— Rachel Caine, Fall of Night

"The boys had always been her reason to stay, but now for the first time they were her reason to leave. She'd allowed violence to become a normal part of their life."

— Liane Moriarty, Big Little Lies

"Don't play his game. Play yours."

-Rachel Caine, Fall of Night

ABOUT THE AUTHOR

Atlanta GA resident with my 4 children ages 5, 4, 3, and 6 months. My children and I are Domestic Violence survivors. Every day we strive to get stronger and learn to love a little harder. I enjoy Helping other victims, and speaking publicly. I raise my children myself, write to inspire, and own a burial at Sea Company. I live my life to the fullest and share love wherever we may go. I share this book in hopes of educating and empowering other victims or loved ones, to understand the cycle of abuse, and that it can happen to anyone. My aspirations are to inspire those stuck in DV relationships to seek help, and to let survivors, who had to learn the hard way, find their own voice once more.

(fin)

Made in the USA
Columbia, SC
25 September 2022